Satan and The Origin of Evil

Gil Stieglitz

Satan and The Origin of Evil
Building Strong Christians for the Battle
© 2015 Gil Stieglitz

Published by Principles to Live By, Roseville CA 95661
www.ptlb.com

Cover by John Chase
Copyedited by Jennifer Edwards

All rights reserved. No part of this publication may be reproduced, stored in a retrieval system, or transmitted in any way by an means-electronic, mechanical, photocopy, recording, or otherwise-without the prior permission of the copyright holder, except as provided by USA copyright law.

Scripture verses are from the New American Standard Bible unless otherwise indicated.

New American Standard Bible: 1995 update.

1995 La Habra, CA: The Lockman Foundation.

ISBN 978-0-9838602-7-3

Christian Living

Printed in the United States of America

Dedication

This book is dedicated to a hero

Melissa Herrmann

for her relentless work in fighting against
the evil of sex trafficking

Contents

Introduction..7
1. The Origin of Evil..13
2. The Corruption of Lucifer.......................................31
3. The Judgment of Satan...43
4. Inside the Mind of Lucifer......................................53
5. Evil Invades the Human Race................................69
6. What Is Satan's Job Now?.......................................85
Conclusion..113
Appendix 1..123
Appendix 2..133
Appendix 3..141
Appendix 4..149
How to Use This Book...157
About the Author..167
Other Resources...169

Introduction

Something is not right about our universe. At first it seems that our world is wonderful, beautiful, and pleasant. Like it is a straightforward place where doing right is rewarded and everyone has a chance at a beautiful life. But there is something else going on here that is destroying this straightforward equation about life. There is a toxic substance that has been introduced to this beautiful world, spoiling it and disrupting its natural order. It is called *evil*.

Evil is destructive. It is a parasite on the good, an unwelcome addition to this world. To be "good" means to make choices and conduct oneself in such a manner that benefits society, others, and self. Evil twists the good impulses and pursues personal gain in some form, even if it is destructive to others, society, and ultimately to oneself. While evil seems impersonal and random, it had a personal beginning. Good and evil are not equal forces forever locked in a battle for supremacy. Good is primary and can survive without evil; but evil needs good to have something to twist, something to corrupt. Evil is a weed that has sprouted in the garden of goodness. It takes the straight path and twists it, growing in the good world at will unless it is specifically resisted. Goodness adds, benefits, and enriches everyone while evil narrows the focus to self. Evil wants to corrupt the good life. It can hide behind respectability and image, controlling only a small part of a person's life. But that small, infected part can ultimately end up destroying everything.

In order to understand how evil seeks to infect your world and life, it is especially instructive to understand the beginnings of evil. The seeds of evil are everywhere, waiting to be watered and encouraged. If we are to understand why life is not the straight-up proposition we think it should be, it is essential to understand the personal beginning of evil and its ongoing spread. To do so, one must understand Satan and the origin of evil.

One of the most famous dialogues in all recorded history takes place between a man named Job and three of his friends who come to console him over the death of his children, the loss of his wealth, and the destruction of his health. Job's friends advocate a simple view of life, which is that people don't suffer for no apparent reason. Therefore, he must have sinned to have all this difficulty rain down on him. Job also embraces this simple orientation to life but knows that he has not personally sinned in any way to merit this oppression. Through it all he takes up an increasingly loud argument with God. The problem is that while having this intense discussion, neither Job nor his friends seem to know about a malevolent figure lurking in the background causing all of Job's troubles. God has rules, processes, and tests that Job and his three friends do not understand. There was evil at work in Job's life and Job was being tested.

If we are going to make sense of our world, we are going to have to understand the personal origin of evil and this lurking figure's continuing propagation of evil. Yes,

Introduction

we are responsible for our choices. Yes, God has created a cause-and-effect world. Yes, governments and other people can thwart what we are trying to do. But there is also a restless, personal evil that is at work behind the scenes looking to bring evil into our life and expand what is already there.

Let's take a look at the origin of evil and this shadowy figure called the Devil and Satan. Five key passages in the Scriptures describe Satan's origins, the birth of evil, and his role: Job 38:7; Ezekiel 28:11-19; Isaiah 14:12-14; Genesis 3:1-7, and Job 1:1-12. Each of these passages provides unique insights about the angelic being we call the Devil and Satan. The Bible's description of the origin of evil and its growth from one being's rebellion to a worldwide phenomenon is important as we try and live in a world filled with evil. Yes, we now have multiple sewers spilling selfishness, rebellion, and evil into our world; but it began at a particular place with a particular person. The Bible accurately records these events and tells us how God has responded. This particular biblical information is of critical importance to the growing Christian. I am amazed at how empowered people are when they understand where evil comes from and what it is designed to do. This book explains the origin of evil and Satan's internal desires.

Let us begin with the first verse of the Bible:

In the beginning God created the heavens and the earth. (Genesis 1:1)

This first statement is a general statement about the beginning of time, space, and matter as well as a summation statement of the creation of the angelic, human, and all forms of biological life. Before the creation there were no angels; there was only God. In eternity past, before the creation, the Triune God enjoyed complete peace within Himself. He did not need to create the universe, angels, or mankind; but He chose to create them. He worked out all the details of His creation before He ever executed the first step of the plan. Nothing that happens in His creation catches Him by surprise even though not everything in His creation pleases him. One of the elements of His creation plan was the creation of angels in their various forms and functions. We know that for some period of time the angels were functioning according to their prescribed roles and responsibility as we read in Job 38:4-7.

> *Where were you when I laid the foundation of the earth? Tell Me, if you have understanding, who set its measurements? Since you know. Or who stretched the line on it? On what were its bases sunk? Or who laid its cornerstone, <u>when the morning stars sang together and all the sons of God shouted for joy?</u>*

Notice that the when the foundations of the earth were laid, all the morning stars sang together and all the sons of God shouted for joy. The morning stars and the sons of God are understood to be the angels. What we can conclude from this passage is that for some period of time, after the initial creation event and through the formation of the earth, there was no rebellion in the angelic ranks. (We come to understand that there is later, however.) Notice that all the sons of God shouted for joy when the earth was formed. This means that the idea of rebellion against God's plan had not yet occurred in the heart of Lucifer -- the highest-ranking angel through which evil was born. His person, rebellion, judgment, and role are detailed in Ezekiel 28:11-19, Isaiah 14:12-14, Genesis 3:1-7, and Job 1:1-12. We will examine each of these passages in depth in the following chapters.

1

The Origin of Evil

Ezekiel 28:11-19

The answer to the question of evil's origin is found in Ezekiel 28:11-19. This prophetic passage is rich in imagery and details about Lucifer and the birth of evil in the universe. Interestingly, evil did not begin where one would think. It did not grow out of the lowly underbelly of the world or emerge from some dark corner of God's creation. It began with the highest-ranking angel in the most bizarre place. Its formation shouldn't have happened at all but it did. It is a tale that boggles the mind. Since evil seeks to jump from host-to-host and will seek to jump to you in the most unusual way, it is best to be prepared. Read on and be amazed.

Begin by reading through Ezekiel 28:11-19 and pay close attention to the information that is revealed about the origin of evil. You will need to read slowly as there is a lot here. Please take the time to underline various words, write questions in the margin, and circle key words as you read.

Again the word of the LORD came to me saying, Son of man, take up a lamentation over the king of Tyre and say to him, 'Thus says the Lord GOD, You had the seal of perfection, full of wisdom and perfect in beauty. You were in Eden, the garden of God; every precious stone was your covering: the ruby, the topaz and the diamond; the beryl, the onyx and the jasper; the lapis lazuli, the turquoise and the emerald; and the gold, the workmanship of your settings and sockets, was in you. On the day that you were created they were prepared. You were the anointed cherub who covers, and I placed you there. You were on the holy mountain of God; you walked in the midst of the stones of fire. You were blameless in your ways from the day you were created until unrighteousness was found in you. By the abundance of your trade you were internally filled with violence, and you sinned; therefore I have cast you as profane from the mountain of God. And I have destroyed you, O covering cherub, from the midst of the stones of fire. Your heart was lifted up because of your beauty; you corrupted your wisdom by reason of your splendor. I cast you to the ground; I put you before kings, that they may see you. By the multitude of your iniquities, in the unrighteousness of your trade you profaned your sanctuaries. Therefore I have brought fire from the midst of you; it has consumed you, and I have turned you to ashes on the earth in the eyes of all who see you. All who know you among the peoples are appalled at you; you have become terrified and you will cease to be forever."

The Origin of Evil

At first glance, it seems that this passage refers directly to the king of Tyre who was referred to in the preceding verses, 1-10. But many conservative evangelical scholars believe verses 11-19 to be a symbolic reference to Satan as the power who influenced the ruler of Tyre. This is because the descriptions are too extreme to refer to a human (You had the seal of perfection; You were the anointed cherub who covers; You were on the holy mountain of God; You were in Eden, the garden of God). When taken literally it can only refer to one being -- the angel we call the Devil and Satan.

When taken from this perspective, we learn a tremendous amount about this powerful angelic being from this passage. This is the creature bent on blocking humans achieving God's design and the abundant life he has for them (Ephesians 2:10). This being is not named in this passage, but in other passages he is identified as Lucifer (Isaiah 14:12-14), Satan (Job 1), and the Devil (1 Peter 5:8). Let's look again at the information we gain about this being in verses 12-15.

> *You had the seal of perfection, full of wisdom and perfect in beauty. You were in Eden, the garden of God; every precious stone was your covering: the ruby, the topaz and the diamond; the beryl, the onyx and the jasper; the lapis lazuli, the turquoise and the emerald; And the gold, the workmanship of your settings and sockets, was in you. On the day that you were created they were prepared. You were the anointed cherub who covers, and I placed you there. You were on the holy mountain of God; you walked in the midst of the stones of fire. You*

were blameless in your ways from the day you were created until unrighteousness was found in you.

This passage includes fourteen insights into this powerful creature, Lucifer. Let me make an explanatory comment about each of them.

You had the seal of perfection

The Hebrew word translated perfection is the word *taknit,* which means "proportioned, perfect, example." If one could imagine what a perfect angel is like, it would be this being. He was the sum total of what it meant to be an angel. He was perfect. What I mean by this is that he was perfectly designed to fulfill the purpose that God had designed for him. In his original position, he was the most powerful angel ever created. He was the ruler over the cherubim who are the highest order of angelic beings. In this position he ruled over all the other angels as well. His perfection in angelic terms did not mean that he was incorruptible, though, as we all know. Of the type of being that angels are, Lucifer was the perfect expression of everything an angel was supposed to be.

Full of wisdom

The Hebrew word translated wisdom is *hacmah,* which means "the ability to apply knowledge." Wisdom is not accumulated knowledge but the ability to accomplish something with that knowledge. It is not that this angelic being had all this heaped up information at his ready; rather, it was that God created Lucifer with an amazing ability to apply knowledge to the situations that he found himself facing. In other words, he was wise in the sense that he could apply knowledge to get a desired result. Nowadays we would call him cunning, manipulative, and treacherous which is just the application of wisdom in a selfish, negative, and destructive way. In his position of rulership over the angels he was capable of taking the facts about the various types of angels, the universe, the spiritual dimensions that the angels dwelt in, and the facts of who God was to administrate his duties in a magnificent way. It is important to realize that wisdom of this sort is capable of engaging in large and complex projects to accomplish the desired result. His ability to accomplish his goals through multiple steps, with multiple players, over multiple years, while damaged by his sinfulness is what makes him so treacherous. Note, however, that he was not omniscient. He did not know everything as God does, but he has the ability to apply what he does know in uniquely clever ways to accomplish his goals. As we shall see, he develops the desire to use his incredible ability to apply knowledge to accomplish his own selfish goals rather than use it for God's purposes and the other angels' benefit.

Perfect in beauty

Not only was this being capable of applying knowledge over vast spans of time with multiple individuals and groups, he was also appealing in every sense of that word. He looked good, sounded good, smelled good, and felt good (if anything got close enough to do that). The idea of "perfect in beauty" means alluring of form with all its proportional dimensions but also perfect in presentation of self to the other angels. We would call this a perfect, magnetic personality that continues to draw you in to his words, ideas, and leadership. When we see something that is beautiful, we are drawn to keep looking at it because our eyes connect with the proportions and colors. While Satan may have sinned, he is still beautiful and understands the power of beauty to retain attention, desire, and control. The angels were drawn to him. He was their ruler and they wanted to be ruled by him.

You were in Eden, the garden of God

This marker or factoid is what convinces us that this passage isn't about a mere mortal. God is talking, through Ezekiel, to the being that animated the serpent in the garden. This is Lucifer, the Devil, and/or Satan. What is interesting here is that Eden is specifically designated as the garden of God. It was not a naturally occurring phenomenon. God put it where it was. He set up the rules for how it functioned and the work that Adam and Eve needed to do to maintain it and extend it. We learn later in one of the other key passages that Lucifer aims at robbing Adam and Eve of their close relationship with God by convincing them that they can become their own gods. Eden was supposed to be the spreading model of the kingdom of God throughout the earth, but the Devil charged in there and destroyed it.

Every precious stone was your covering

He was meant to reflect the light of God to the angelic realms in its brilliance, radiance, and different hues. A direct and constant vision of God was not possible even for the angels; they needed to have God mediated to them through the reflected glory off this being. Just like we can't stare at the sun but can look at the moon, the angels could not look directly at the unapproachable light of God (1 Timothy 6:18). However, they could discern the wonder of God by the creation and covering of Lucifer.

The ruby, the topaz and the diamond, the beryl, the onyx and the jasper, the lapis lazuli, the turquoise and the emerald

There have been various suggestions as to the exact meaning of these stones, but all of these types of symbolic renderings of individual stones lack specificity. It is more helpful to note that each of these stones, both in the ancient and modern world, bring out a different color and hue of light. It is more helpful and less fanciful to tie these stones to the idea of reflections of various aspects of the glory of God. This angel's coverings were designed to reflect the light of the glory of God and show aspects of His being that could not be seen in just the blinding white light of His presence. Lucifer was not the source of the light but was a refractive and reflective surface for the display of the wonder of God. It's sad that it wasn't enough for him. He was in an incredibly privileged place and yet there was a desire for more. If wanting more of a spotlight could corrupt the highest angelic being set in a supremely exalted place, then we must push for more humility and realize that no amount of power or fame will ever be enough.

And the gold, the workmanship of your setting and sockets, was in you

This phrase "your settings and sockets" (armor) refers to the clothing that Lucifer wore, not his person. The suit that Lucifer was given to wear was magnificent and showed the presence of God in its design, function, and beauty. Gold is consistently symbolic of the presence of God. God showed himself through all the aspects of Lucifer's garments and vestments. It was clear to the angels that God was magnificent. Lucifer was created as a perfect mirror that displayed the wonder of God; but the mirror itself wanted to be noticed, not just do its function.

On the day that you were created they were prepared

This verse confirms what we said earlier that Lucifer was created and was not a part of eternity with God before the beginning of the universe. The angels were created as a part of the running of the universe that God created. Lucifer is a created being and his suit was made on the same day that this high angel was created. There was never going to be a time when Lucifer was separated from the suit that would reflect the glory of God. There was never going to be a time when Lucifer could be "himself" without the reflected glory of God. This inability to separate himself from the glory of God eventually became too much for him and he rebelled. He wanted the spotlight personally. He wanted to command attention to himself. He wanted to be selfish rather than enjoy the wonder of how God made him and what God made him for. This is always at the heart of sin.

You were the anointed cherub who covers

There are four specific types of angels that are mentioned in the Scriptures: Cherubim, Seraphim, Archangels, and Angels. Some Christian groups have identified more separate groups of angels, but the scriptural evidence is ambiguous at best. Cherubim are considered the highest order of angelic beings. In the first chapter of this same book (Ezekiel), the prophets' description of the vision of God and the wheels describes four living creatures which are usually described as cherubim (Ezekiel 1:5-24). These beings correspond to the cherubim mentioned in Ezekiel 10:2-22. The cherubim are the angels that cover the mercy seat which is the top of the Ark of the Covenant (Exodus 25:17-22). These are identified usually as the living creatures in the book of Revelation that administrate the unfolding plan of God's redemption. They have a level of power and wisdom not seen in the other angels. According to this verse, Lucifer's role was to be the highest angel covering the other cherubim and the other angels. Remember, God's authority structure is different than mankind's authority structure. Those who lead serve the most. Therefore, Lucifer had the privilege of serving the cherubim and the whole angelic host. It was an exalted servant role from which he eventually rebelled. He wanted to be served instead of to serve.

And I placed you there

God put Lucifer in his position. This was not an earned position. God designed, created, and placed a special angel in this supreme position of privilege and responsibility. This phrase emphasizes that God specifically did the placing. This was not a choice that Lucifer made. This was not a merited assignment because he beat out the other angels. This was not a role he grew into. He had been specifically designed to do this role by God and then rejected the assignment after serving in the capacity for some period of time. He was perfectly suited for a particular role and allowed his own selfishness to lure him out of that role in search for greater self-focus and greater control. How foolish! In the same way our heart is desperately wicked and whispers to us that the perfect family, the perfect job, the perfect level of influence is not enough. Our own heart tells us we can do better and pushes us to rebellion and destruction to get it.

You were the on the holy mountain of God

This seems to be a reference of direct access into the presence of God. Lucifer had access to the holiness and wonder of God that was not true of the other angels. He interacted directly with LIFE itself. Imagine the privilege of this interaction. This is the privilege that we will know in heaven one day when we dwell in the celestial city. We will have access to the holy mountain of God. We will be in God's direct, unmediated presence. In his epic poem, *Paradise Lost,* Milton suggests that Lucifer became aware of God's plan to create and redeem mankind -- a creature significantly inferior to the angelic realm. This

The Origin of Evil

information caused him to rebel. It's an interesting idea, but we have a more direct revelation that tells us that it was his pride and rebellion in his role that gave birth to the sin in his heart.

You walked in the midst of the stones of fire

This seems to be a reference to the undulating attributes and aspects of the person of God. It is a deeper reference to Lucifer's access into God's presence. The stones seem to be a representation of the glory of God in its glowing brilliance. The angels needed to have the glory of God stepped down to them through the suit that Lucifer was fitted to wear, but he himself was able to move among the actual glow of the glory of God. He had this level of perfection, power, and privilege; and yet he threw it all away by chasing what he already had.

You were blameless in your ways

It is clear from this statement that Lucifer was not flawed in any way. The original impetus for evil arose out of his own thoughts, not from some fault that can be charged to God. God created a world where evil was possible but not necessary. Evil originated in Lucifer, not in God. Lucifer had an incredible place of privilege and power which had been specifically designed to fit him perfectly. God puts the responsibility on Lucifer for the choices that he made. He reminds him of the facts, and in this way reiterates the truth of Galatians 6:7 even in the angelic realm, "Do not be deceived, God is not mocked;

for whatever a man sows, this he will also reap." We are responsible; we don't have to sin.

From the day you were created until unrighteousness was found in you

One of the saddest verses in all of the Scriptures is recorded here. Unrighteousness was found in this perfect being and, thus the flow of evil starts. Instead of a continued focus on adding, benefiting, and blessing God, the whole of creatures in the universe, his angelic kind, and himself, this angel twisted the good impulse and put himself in the primary place. He did not care what happened to others as long as he got what he wanted. Self-focus begins and spreads death and destruction in its wake. Evil originated in the mind of Lucifer, not in the plan of God. Did God know that it would happen? Clearly, yes! But evil's creation was from Lucifer, not God. It is amazing that just a slight twisting of where the primary focus of benefit, blessing, and reward should lie could create such a trail of destruction. I hear this all the time: "I didn't mean for any of this to happen." "I just wanted to do what seemed right to me." Evil twists the good with a primary focus on self. Doing good can stand alone when we ask the question, "Does everyone benefit?" If the answer is "yes," then proceed. If only you or a small group of people are the only ones who benefit, or if others will be damaged or destroyed by this action, then stop -- it is evil. One is sobered by the Devil's story. If the perfect job with stunning perks and over-the-top abilities is not sufficient to hold us in righteousness, we should all feel stunned. Pride is so much more dangerous of a thing than we will ever be able to fully comprehend. Yet, we catch a glimpse of its devastation here. All the murders, all the rapes, all the tyranny, and all the abuse flow from this one act. When you put yourself at the center of what needs to happen "no matter what," then evil has jumped to another host.

At this point, let's transition to application of what we have just learned. How does this affect our life? What are we supposed to do with it? What does God want me to do with this information specifically? The next section is a series of spiritual exercises that will help you apply the material you just learned about. There may be other applications but these have been included to bring these truths into your life in a practical way.

Spiritual Exercise

Begin with confession

Confess your pride of trying to build a life without the Lord and without His designs. Ask God to show you the ways that your self-focus and ego have led you to trust in the wrong people, the wrong activities, and the wrong pleasures. Confess to the Lord your pursuit of your own desires above what was beneficial for everyone in your life.

Did your self-focus push you to grasp after vengeance, drugs, alcohol, power, fame, money, sex, gambling, get-rich-quick schemes, laziness, food, or rage instead of staying with the path of righteousness that God wanted you to pursue?

Move to repentance

Let's have a "come to Jesus" meeting about how much you are like the Devil and have tried to build your world around your screwy ideas instead of God's ideas. Lucifer thought his life would improve if he were free of God's restrictions, God's rules, and God's responsibilities. He was wrong just as you are wrong when you try and do the same thing. The Devil has never repented of his foolish opinion, but you can.

Right now, declare to God that you realize your rebellious ideas for your life are not helpful, wise, or productive. You can pray a prayer like this:

"Oh God, I have been so wrong! I thought I was so wise, and yet, I was a fool just like the Devil. I thought I had a better plan than the one you had for me. I repent. I change my mind and I want to follow your lead. I want to live in the center of your will instead of the center of my ego. You were right and I was wrong. I chose poorly. I chose selfishly. I moved away from the life that you had planned for me. I did not trust you to lead me to green pastures and still waters. I did not trust that you had my best interests at heart. I was wrong."

The Origin of Evil

"Please forgive me for my willfulness and rebellion. Please apply the blood of Jesus Christ to my selfishness and stupidity. Please show me how to utilize the skills, talents, gifts, and dreams that you have put within me."

In the Name of the Lord Jesus Christ,

Amen

Spiritual Exercise

Examine God's provision for your life

What gifts, talents, abilities, dreams, and opportunities have you been given? Yes, write them down.

Take stock of the gifts of the Lord. These gifts usually point in a direction and suggest how God wants to use you to glorify Him. Are you using your gifts, talents, abilities, and opportunities now? Have you allowed something, someone, or some evil to turn you away from doing what your were made to do or being who you are? What would it look like if you were to press deeper into the person God made you to be? Again, write it down.

When I work with people who have surrendered to sin, evil, and/or Satan in profound ways, I always find a person who is unfulfilled and miserable. The music that they were meant to create and play is still in them. They were meant to do something, be something, and create something. Their future was stolen from them because they were seduced into following something, someone, or some group that said there was a shortcut to a better future. The Devil fell for an idea that he could be more if he went against what God was offering. He discovered, as everyone who falls for this lie discovers, it is not true. Your best self, your best life, and your best relationships come from you being the real you, the talented you, the productive you that God created.

One of the first things we must talk about is what were you meant to do. What is the dream that is hidden in your heart? If you are going to break free from the grip of sin and Satan, you must begin to dream again about fulfilling the person you truly are. It doesn't matter whether you are in a prison cell, a lousy job, or in a bad marriage, the person God made you still needs to come out.

What is your righteous dream? How could you take a step towards that dream? Your righteous dream has a way of being expressed no matter how damaged your life has become. It is the dream that will light the way, and in many ways, generate the power to get there. Write out your dream here:

The Origin of Evil

What is the righteous dream for your spiritual life?

What is the righteous dream for your personal life?

What is the righteous dream for your marital life?

What is the righteous dream for your family?

What is the righteous dream for your career and vocation?

What is the righteous dream for your finances and resources?

What is the righteous dream for society and your involvement in it?

What is the righteous dream for your friends?

Yes, I know that the righteous dream may look a little different now than when you first envisioned it, but write it down and let's get started moving in that direction.

2

The Corruption of Lucifer
Ezekiel 28:16-17a

The prophet Ezekiel goes on to tell us more of what happened to Lucifer to bring about his corruption in verses 28:16-17a. God outlines what was taking place in the heavens and how it corrupted Lucifer. He also describes Satan's immediate and future judgment.

> *By the abundance of your trade you were internally filled with violence, and you sinned; therefore I have cast you as profane from the mountain of God. And I have destroyed you, O covering cherub, from the midst of the stones of fire. Your heart was lifted up because of your beauty; you corrupted your wisdom by reason of your splendor. I cast you to the ground;*

Let's take a more detailed look at each of the further statements about Lucifer's sin and judgment.

By the abundance of your trade you were internally filled with violence, and you sinned

This describes one of the functions of Lucifer as the anointed cherub who covers and how that specific function led him into pride and corruption of his exalted position. Remember, he was perfectly made and equipped to do his role. This was an important and exalted position. God tells us that it was the amount of trade that Lucifer was involved in that brought out the corruption. It seems from what we have already seen of the description of Lucifer that he was the middleman between God and the angelic host. He covered the angels from the brilliance and holiness of God which they could not handle directly (just as we cannot handle it directly, 1 Timothy 6:16), and he mediated the praise and glory of the angels back to God. In other words, he was some kind of go-between, mediator, or translator between the Almighty God and the angels. It is this trade that led to his downfall. Imagine the amount of "trade" that took place in the heavenlies between God and the angels. Somewhere the privilege of being on the mountain of God, in the midst of the stones of fire, translating, mediating, and radiating the glory of God out to the angels and then receiving the praise, adoration, and thanksgiving of the angels toward God, he decided he wanted to keep some of God's glory for himself. He was less than God, clearly, but he was more than the other angels. He began to receive the praise of the angels as directed at himself instead of passing it on to God. He began to imagine that the radiated glory, wonder, and power of God was coming from him instead of passing through him. He was the moon, yet he began to think of himself as the sun.

This is where evil began in the universe. I realize that this is an amazing thing to say, so let me say it again. *This is where evil began in the universe.* Before this point in time, evil did not exist. It was birthed in the heart of a being who became so excessively self-focused, rather than staying God-focused, that he threw away everything he had been given and accomplished in order to gain a ludicrous imaginary goal. It is with amazing clarity that God reveals to us that evil is birthed and resides in the self-focused heart. That is why God declares through Solomon that pride is an abomination to him (Proverbs 16:5).

Evil ravages individuals, families, communities, and nations but here is where it starts. This is where evil always starts. Selfishness is the little spring that gives birth to evil. All of the destructiveness that evil eventually becomes flows out of this small, very personal beginning: "I want what I want and I am willing to do what I have to do to get it." When a person's individual desires trump other people's needs and/or when they trump God's rules, laws, and plans, then evil begins. How strongly evil flows from any one individual depends upon how relentless they are in their pursuit of their own selfish desires.

It is not wrong to explore new possibilities mentally; in fact, it should be encouraged. But one has to always ask the question: Does everyone benefit from this action or choice? Exploring new possibilities are the way that society progresses and fulfills God's desire to multiply and fill the earth. But if the only person who benefits is the individual proposing it, then it is evil no matter how slick it is presented. Oftentimes, new ideas can be tweaked and adjusted so that all can benefit, not just a few.

We do not usually recognize evil until it becomes destructive to others, the individual themselves, and/or to the society at large. This is the classic definition of evil: doing harm to others in order to get what you want. This is what the Bible calls *wickedness*. It should be obvious that evil can come in a number of forms: personal, financial, mental, emotional, sexual, power, fame, prestige, and so on. It has been the specific function of governments to find and restrict behavior that harms others while it enriches a few. But in every culture and every time period people have become blind to certain evils and certain injustices. This is why God is clear that when a process, business, system, person, or group is involved in profiting at the destruction or damage of others, it must be stopped, without pity. This search for injustice, oppression, and evil is a never-ending battle because evil can grow in the heart of every single person.

The root of evil is capable of springing up in anyone and spreading from there. How big your ego is determines how far you push down the road of evil. Righteousness necessitates a God-focus; an others-focus, as well as an awareness of self. Righteousness recognizes that you are not the center of the universe.

We see this process in business, sports, families, and nations all the time. A person who has gifts and abilities does something good and they begin to believe that they did it all. They are not a part of a team. They don't need others. They aren't a part of the solution; they *are* the solution. They stop realizing all the factors and people that brought them to the place where they could play their crucial part. Pride enters their heart and it becomes about them. They become self-focused. There is nothing wrong with enjoying the special skills, contributions, and the impact that you can make; but it

The Corruption of Lucifer

is always a result of far more than just you. Aren't we always impressed when a person does something great or gets a promotion and does not let it go to their head? They keep making their contribution realizing that there are a lot of other people who also must make their unique contribution in order for them to succeed.

Lucifer became convinced that he was more than he actually was. He became enamored with receiving praise, adoration, and accolades. It is clear that although he walked in the midst of the stones of fire and on the mountain of God, he became convinced that he deserved this praise even to the place where he wanted to be like God. But he did not comprehend the height, depth, or width of the wonder of God. He became familiar with an aspect of God and began to disrespect God because of his familiarity. Even Lucifer -- this specially created angel -- could not comprehend the majesty and wonder of the Almighty.

Therefore I have cast you as profane from the mountain of God

When Lucifer either embraced the thoughts that he had created or acted upon his feelings of superiority in some way, God acted. God threw him out of the mountain of God. He couldn't be there anymore. Something had changed in Lucifer and God immediately knew it. He was no longer the servant fulfilling his ordained role. He was a rival considering himself as an equal. He had to go. He was corrupting the sanctuary of God with his thoughts. Lucifer could no longer be trusted with the privilege of being in the stones of fire and on the mountain of God. We can clearly see the folly of Lucifer's miscomprehension of his abilities and wisdom. There was no way that Lucifer was even close to equal with

God, but he was deceived by his own focus on his own gifts. He was looking at how much he knew and what he could do instead of all God knows, is, and is able to do. We can get caught in the same trap of believing we are more than we actually are and begin to edge God out of the center of our lives. My friends in the recovery world tell me this is the definition of EGO -- Edging God Out.

Notice that the judgment of Lucifer began to take place back at that point. Lucifer was diminished. He could no longer move onto the mountain of God and into the stones of fire as he could before. We see his diminished position in the first chapter of Job where Lucifer has been roaming around on the earth and is granted access to talk with God again at God's request. We will explore more of his judgment through the next few statements but realize that Satan has been judged, is being judged, and will be judged. To us he is powerful and menacing and even in his diminished capacity he is, but he has been judged and is waiting for a final judgment that is described in this passage.

And I have destroyed you, O covering cherub, from the midst of the stones of fire

What Lucifer once was, he is no longer. He has been destroyed in terms of his original purpose, design, and function. We do not know whether there is another angelic being that took over his duties, but he can no longer do them. He is destroyed in that role. Something about what he did and what he was as the covering cherub is destroyed.

There is too much thinking in Christian circles that the Devil rebelled from God and ran away to set up a hidden base of operation where he launches attacks on God's people. This is not what happened at all. And it is not happening that way now. God destroyed the Devil from his position as anointed cherub as a partial judgment. God has further judgments for the Devil in the future. The Devil, in his corrupted state, is fulfilling a unique purpose that God has for him. The Lord knows exactly where the Devil is and what he is doing at any given moment. He is under God's mandated judgment.

Your heart was lifted up because of your beauty

This statement about what was going on in the soul of Lucifer is extremely telling. It declares the nature of his self-focus. He allowed himself to think too highly of himself because of the perfection of his proportions. His own beauty corrupted him. Beauty is a function of proportion. When things are in the right proportion -- whether architecture or color -- our eyes perceive that as beautiful. When something is out of proportion, then it is less beautiful or not beautiful. It was God who designed Lucifer's proportions and therefore God who deserved the credit for his beauty. But Lucifer ignored all of that and instead acted and thought as though he earned the accolades -- that he deserved the praise. God is cutting to the heart of Lucifer's problem. He embraced God's gifts in a corrupting way and his self-focus destroyed him. Once he made these choices he would never be the same again. He had been destroyed and would be destroyed even further.

It is so easy to follow in the sin of Lucifer and be lifted up with pride because of things that were given to us by God and others. The gifted athlete becomes proud instead of thanking

God, his parents, and his coaches. His whole world tells him that he is wonderful because of his ability to throw, run, catch, block, or skate. Everyone says *yes* to him because of these skills, and he embraces this influence to his own corruption. The beautiful young woman begins to own her beauty in her mind like Lucifer did here and uses her beauty to extend power over others. People bend to her desires because of her beauty and she internalizes this power as her own. She becomes corrupted. The brilliant student believes that they worked, earned, or deserved their facility with math, computers, science, or art. He or she focuses on how others are beneath them in this area, and they embrace this hierarchy as the way the whole world should work. They are corrupted by an endowment from God.

You corrupted your wisdom by reason of your splendor

This is another deeply pregnant statement. Lucifer's ability to apply knowledge to administrate the world and potentially the universe was corrupted because of his self-focus on his proportions (his beauty). His thoughts became about himself and how to showcase them to increase his power. Wisdom is about applying knowledge so that God wins, others win, and you win; but he focused on his own personal win. When wisdom becomes corrupted enough, it fights for a personal win at great cost to others and great cost to God. This is what the Devil did. He used his wisdom to deceive the angels into following him even though it would mean their judgment. All Lucifer was thinking about was his own exaltation at that moment. Applied knowledge can be corrupted when it is used to gain at others' expense. This is called wickedness in the Bible. If I gain at your expense, then

The Corruption of Lucifer

I am using wisdom in a corrupt way. True wisdom finds a way for everybody to win.

Just like with Satan, we can immediately think of a number of ways to gain personally but which entail damage or destruction for others. These wicked ways must be turned away from because it is not righteous. Wickedness will eventually consume those who gain in these ways. There is always a way to gain which includes gain for everyone; it just takes more searching and a willingness to embrace lower or longer-term personal gains.

I cast you to the ground

There seem to be two ideas potentially in this statement. First, that he could no longer fly or propel himself through the eternal dimensions after this judgment. He could, in the past, move in the dimensionality of eternity with ease but now is confined. He has been grounded. Most commentators represent this as being restricted from access to the third heaven while still maintaining power and mobility in the second and first heavens. What once was his privilege has been stripped away from him. Second, this grounding suggests that he is restricted to this earth in some way and no longer has unrestricted access to the eternal dimensions. His confinement is to or around this earth. This is also stated in Isaiah 14:12-15 when it is said about Lucifer,

> *How you have fallen from heaven, O star of the morning, son of the dawn! You have been cut down to the earth.*

There is some type of clear judgment that has taken place on Lucifer in that some of the privilege and power he had before has been removed from him. Lucifer has been restricted and his work has been changed from what it was to what it now is. We see this restriction on Satan in Job 1.

> *Now there was a day when the sons of God came to present themselves before the LORD, and Satan also came among them. The LORD said to Satan, "From where do you come?" Then Satan answered the LORD and said,* ***"From roaming about on the earth and walking around on it"*** (Job 1:6, 7).

Satan was roaming around on the earth rather than moving among the eternal realms freely. His job changed from its original assignment. His being cast down is seen. The Devil is not in charge of angels, and he is not going into God's presence. Satan has a significantly reduced role in God's world and greatly reduced access to God.

Again it is time to transition to a time of application. What does this information mean to me? How am I supposed to use this material? In what ways can I change my life to be in line with these truths? Various spiritual exercises have been included to help facilitate applying this information.

Spiritual Exercise

Examine your level of self-focus

In what ways have you followed Lucifer and allowed your gifts, abilities, privilege, or position to decrease your dependence upon God? Has your EGO been allowed to "Edge God Out" in some way?

Sometimes this self-focus takes the form that it took with the Devil (I am great; I am being limited; I should have more freedom, more responsibility, more attention, etc.). Is this your tendency?

Sometimes a self-focus takes a negative form where a person becomes a hypochondriac, a cynic, or a pessimist, constantly complaining about how the world is not meeting their needs, making them comfortable, or allowing them to be successful. This negative way is often called a "victim mentality." This person sees the whole world through the selfish prism of his or her own wants. (There is a bigger world out there than just your immediate desires.) Is this your tendency?

Both directions are self-focused and both are deadly in accomplishing a great life. Acknowledge all that God gave you. Give thanks for your gifts, your opportunities, your heritage, and your opportunities. Spend some actual time giving thanks to God for these things. Take responsibility for your mess-ups and your missed opportunities. Tell God that you realize that without Him and His plan, your life will not be all that it can be. Without Him, your life will be like the Devil - a sewer life, doomed to less than it could be.

Spiritual Exercise

Allow for God's forgiveness

If you have been limited or reduced because of choices that you have made or others have made for you, acknowledge those realities and judgments.

Embrace the wonder of forgiveness that God extends to humanity that He did not extend to the angels. God gives grace, mercy, and redemption to humans who are willing to receive these things from Him (1 Peter 1:12; Romans 5:8, 8:1; Ephesians 2:8,9).

3

The Judgment of Satan
Ezekiel 28:17b-19

The judgment of Satan is detailed in several places in Scripture. Ezekiel 28 speaks of a "grounding" which is clearly a judgment of Lucifer and all those who followed him in rebellion. Another grounding judgment is found in Revelation 12:4a, which tells us that one-third of the angels followed him in his rebellion against God and were likewise judged with Lucifer:

> *And his tail swept away a third of the stars of heaven and threw them to the earth.*

In this verse the dragon is mentioned as being involved in throwing a third of the stars to the ground. In the passage in Ezekiel only Lucifer is mentioned as being grounded. God judged Lucifer for his thoughts and actions of rebellion. Through his recruitment of a third of the angels he was involved in the judgment on the other angels. There will be further judgments upon Lucifer and the other angels beyond the confinement to this planet. They will eventually be judged and confined to the bottomless pit as mentioned in Revelation

20:2,3. This judgment will be for a thousand-year period of time. After that time Lucifer and the other corrupted angels will again be loosed so they can be allowed to deceive those who want to be deceived for another period of time. Finally, they will be thrown into the lake of fire as their final judgment (Revelation 20:10).

The Bible Knowledge Commentary puts it this way:

> Though Ezekiel presented the fall of Satan as a single act, it actually occurred in stages. Satan's initial judgment was his expulsion from the position of God's anointed cherub before His throne. God expelled him from the mount of God (heaven, v. 16; cf. v. 14). Satan was cast from God's government in heaven (cf. Luke 10:18) but was still allowed access to God (cf. Job 1:6–12; Zech. 3:1–2). In the Tribulation, Satan will be cast from heaven and restricted to the earth (Rev. 12:7–13); in the Millennium he will be in the bottomless pit (Rev. 20:1–3); and after his brief release at the end of the Millennium (Rev. 20:7–9) he will be cast into the lake of fire forever (Rev. 20:10).[1]

---

[1] Dyer, C. H. (1985). Ezekiel. In J. F. Walvoord & R. B. Zuck (Eds.), *The Bible Knowledge Commentary: An Exposition of the Scriptures* (Vol. 1, p. 1284). Wheaton, IL: Victor Books.

The Judgment of Satan

Ezekiel 28:17b-19 let us look further into Satan's future judgment with four sentences. Most conservative scholars see these statements as judgments that are yet future versus the grounding judgment described in Ezekiel 28:17a. The Devil has been judged, but his judgment will be completed after he has filled out the full measure of his corruption.

> *I put you before kings, that they may see you. By the multitude of your iniquities, in the unrighteousness of your trade you profaned your sanctuaries. Therefore I have brought fire from the midst of you; it has consumed you, and I have turned you to ashes on the earth In the eyes of all who see you. All who know you among the peoples are appalled at you; you have become terrified and you will cease to be forever.*

Let's take a more detailed look at each of the four statements about Lucifer's future judgment.

I put you before kings, that they may see you

This seems to be a reference to a display of this judged angelic being before leaders of nations and cities. It seems best to understand this as a further elucidation of his judgment. The anointed cherub, who covered all the angels and walked in the presence of the Almighty, was judged and made to interact with human rulers instead of the exalted majesties he had been dealing with. This was quite a come down for this ruler of the angels. His power was now working to influence puny human rulers and their puny human realms.

By the multitude of your iniquities, in the unrighteousness of your trade you profaned your sanctuaries

God again mentions Satan's transgressions which revolve around the display of God's glory and the translation of the praise of the angels. Lucifer was placed by God at the center of that "trade," and he could not handle the volume and magnificence of it all. It is much like those who work at the Treasury Department. If they think of their job as just counting slips of paper, then they are fine; but if they begin to focus on the fact that they are counting real money, then their job will mess with them and they will cease to be an effective Treasury agent. Lucifer was a created being who had a job to do. It was a special job and he was specially designed and equipped to do it. But what he was doing got to him and he became self-focused. He ceased to be a servant doing an important job and he became, in his own mind, worthy of so much more because he was doing this job. Let us make sure that we do not think more highly of ourselves than we ought to think but to think soberly, realistically, as to have sound judgment (Romans 12:3).

Therefore I have brought fire from the midst of you; it has consumed you, and I have turned you to ashes on the earth in the eyes of all who see you

This statement is a predictive prophecy of the final judgment of Lucifer that is yet future. God will confine Lucifer and the angels that followed him in the Lake of Fire and bring the fire out of the midst of them. It will consume them. We read about this in Revelation 20:10, *And the devil who deceived them was thrown into the lake of fire and brimstone,*

The Judgment of Satan

where the beast and the false prophet are also; and they will be tormented day and night forever and ever.

All who know you among the peoples are appalled at you; you have become terrified. And you will cease to be forever

This is a very interesting description of the final end of Satan, the one who produced fear and terror in so many. He will be terrified by the final triumph of righteousness in his life. This end of the one who started all of this sin is important. The one who birthed sin in his own heart allowed himself to think he was worthy of more than the magnificence that God created for him. There is nothing more magnificent and delightful than doing what God created you to do. We give birth to all kinds of sin when we think there is some Shangri-La out there beyond God's design. There is so much in God's design, but there is only death and destruction beyond it. Explore the wonder of who God made you to be. Maximize it but don't embrace the lie that you can be more without God or beyond His plan. Adam and Eve fell for this lie also, plunging all of us into the mess we have today.

It is also instructive that God says in this passage that the Devil will cease to be forever. This is the final judgment of Lucifer. His existence within the universe is over at this final judgment. The Hebrew word *ayin* is used, which means to no longer exist, to cease to be. This brings up an interesting dilemma in that other passages tell us that the Devil and his angels will be tormented forever and ever (Revelation 20:10). Whatever dimensionality of time that is the Lake of Fire, both of these statements are true. He will cease to be and he will be tormented forever. The Lake of Fire may operate as a place of hyper-time in which different rules for existence and time are true. It may also be that the Lake of Fire exists outside of our universe in some way and, therefore, those in it cease to exist and yet still are.

Notice that Lucifer went from the most privileged created being ever to one that will not exist within time and spatial dimensions of our universe. This is quite a fall. His judgment has been in stages. And with the significant diminishment of status and power, he will just not matter anymore because he will be outside of the plane of existence in this world.

Spiritual Exercise

One of the great truths of Christianity is that no one gets away with evil. If they do not receive justice in this life, then they will receive it in the next life. Something in our being cries out for justice. We are seeing a number of famous people (entertainers, politicians, authors, moralists, etc.) who were upheld as good people but are now revealing a dark, evil, and monstrous side. They hid their evil, but it is being revealed even before the fires of the next life. This destructive wickedness must be rewarded with justice.

A verse of Scripture that is not taught much anymore is Galatians 6:7, which states: *Do not be deceived. God is not mocked, for whatever a man sows this he will also reap.* It was true for the Devil and it is true for mankind. There are consequences to our decisions and actions. The Devil has been judged and will be finally and completely judged at some point in the future. His corruption will be completely contained in the Lake of Fire. If a person does not repent of their deeds and plead for the mercy of Jesus Christ, they will be corralled with the Devil and his rebellious angels in the eternal torments of the Lake of Fire. Corruption calls for justice.

Handing over justice to God

God tells us to hand all vengeance over to Him and let Him figure out who, what, how much, and when the person will receive justice (Deuteronomy 32:35; Romans 12:19). We were not meant to carry bitterness, vengeance, and hatred. It rots our soul. Is there anyone who you believe deserves justice but has not received it yet? Pray a prayer of release to the justice of God.

Dear Heavenly Father,

I come in the name of the Lord Jesus Christ and officially hand over to You the justice that is due _____ _____. I believe that they are guilty and deserve punishment, but You have asked me to forgive them and let You handle issues of justice, directly or through Your appointed representatives. You want to free me of the burden of meting out justice to them. You want to free me of the toxic substances of bitterness, hatred, and vengeance. You want to free me to live a life that looks forward and seizes all the opportunities instead of always looking backward focusing on what happened to me. I give all my hate to You. I give all my bitterness to You about what might have been. I want to notice the subtle ways You are leading me to new opportunities. I want to allow what happened to me to become like fertilizer, helping me grow to the next level as a wise person. I want to soon be living a life in which I can almost thank You for the good that You have been able to bring out of the tragedy of what they did.

Love,

Your child _____

In Jesus Christ's Name, Amen

Repent of personal wrongdoing

If there is something that you are doing that you know to be a compromise in righteousness, turn away from it and let it go. Admit that it is wrong and stop sowing seeds of bitterness and death in your life for things you've done or for things others have done to you. Don't be fooled into believing that God doesn't see and that there won't be any penalty to pay. God knew of the Devil's rebellion even before it was a thought. He allowed the Devil the right to choose the wrong course of action. The Devil has not been offered forgiveness but we have. Let us make sure that we do not neglect so great a salvation as the writer of Hebrews tells us.

The Judgment of Satan

Dear Heavenly Father,

I come to you in the name of the Lord Jesus Christ and admit that I need to change my mind about what I have been thinking and doing. I no longer see _____ as good, helpful, or even shrewd. I choose to see and understand _____ as unhelpful, destructive, sinful, and evil. Please allow me to renew my mind so I can get further and further away from even thinking about acting in the way I have in the past.

In the Name of the Lord Jesus Christ,

Amen

4

Inside the Mind of Lucifer
Isaiah 14:12-14

This next passage continues to draw our attention concerning the origin of evil and it's beginning in the mind of Satan. Isaiah 14:12-15 is speaking of the king of Babylon, but begins to describe a person of much greater proportions in verses 12-14. Many commentators on the Scriptures down through the ages have understood this as a reference to the thinking of Lucifer. Through the lips of the prophet Isaiah, this passage is the revelation of what Lucifer was thinking that led him to rebel from all that God had provided. Satan is referred to as the "star of the morning" (Lucifer), and the one who has fallen a great distance. The intimate thoughts of the Devil are described as he leads the assault on God's throne. He wants to be God. Each of his desires can be echoed in the lives of those who follow him. They may dream on a different scale, but they have desires to be like God, to rule others, and to be their own god.

> *How you have fallen from heaven, O star of the morning, son of the dawn! You have been cut down to the earth, you who have weakened the nations!*

> *But you said in your heart, "I will ascend to heaven; I will raise my throne above the stars of God, and I will sit on the mount of assembly in the recesses of the north. I will ascend above the heights of the clouds; I will make myself like the Most High"* (Isaiah 14:12-14).

Let's look at these verses more closely to get a better understanding of how Lucifer's mind was the origin of evil.

How you have fallen from heaven, O star of the morning, son of the dawn

This is a description of the level of descent that Lucifer experienced from where he was and what he was doing to where he is now and what he is doing now. He was the anointed cherub who covered, the highest, most beautiful and wise creature ever created. He was allowed access into the presence of God and given the equipment to accurately reflect the attributes, nature, and essence of God to the angels. From this exalted place he is now confined to earth with limited access to the eternal realms. He is now in charge of testing humanity and bringing consequences on those who fail the tests. The comedown is quite severe. He was exalted, ruling over everything and every being everywhere with great freedom within the broad boundaries of God. He is now ruling over only corrupted angels and corrupted humans. Now, under stringent controls, he tests humans for character, morality, and development. If they fail or fail to seek God's forgiveness for their failures, he is then commissioned with enacting consequences and control over another corrupted human individual. He is working in the backwater of the universe on the worst of humanity. How great is this fall?

You have been cut down to the earth

This is an announcement to everyone that Satan has experienced a significant judgment. He has been confined from unfettered access in the heavenlies to only the earthly realms. The Devil is not all-powerful. The Devil is not omnipresent. The Devil is not sovereign. God is all of these things and so much more and He has judged the Devil for his plot. Notice the word "cut down." This is a forcible reduction in access, position, role, and place. There are other forcible reductions coming later (Revelation 20) that will complete this judgment. But this being cut down to the earth is extremely significant.

You who have weakened the nations

The Devil has been behind the scenes corrupting leaders and nations from pursuing the most powerful agendas. He has weakened the nations by weakening and distracting leaders. The influence for good combined with the power they have been given has been redirected into pursuits of pleasure, money, ego, and rivalry. The Devil has tested the leaders, and the nations have been weakened because of the choices of the leaders.

But you said in your heart

All sin begins in the mind. A person must think of sin and embrace that sin in their mind before it can ever become an action. That is why God goes to the trouble to tell us how evil was birthed in the universe. This rebellious thought pattern has been repeated over and over again millions of times as evil has spread. God describes in detail the goals and the rebellious thoughts that were allowed to take root in Lucifer's mind. It is important to note that these thoughts did not become sin until he embraced them and went to work embellishing them. It is not sinning to be tempted, but it is a sin to embrace and act upon temptations even in your own mind.

The thoughts that actually gave birth to evil were significant enough for God to record them for us so we can look at the way all this evil began. It began when one being allowed himself to embrace the idea that he would make a better god for his life than the real God. Remember, he had been created with incredible gifts, skills, and abilities; and he had been equipped with magnificent gear to accomplish a truly one-of-a-kind function. He was the anointed cherub that covered the angels. He was the go-between, translating the wonder of God to the angels and the praise of the angels back to the Almighty. There was no greater exalted position.

Contentment is a huge attainment. For those with significant gifts, the temptation will always be to think more highly of oneself than one ought to think. It is through dependence on God that we really gain our independence. If God has given you a job, then do it with all your might and find your joy in it. But the germ of sin presented itself to Satan and prompted independence and greater glory by rebelling from the present authority. This is never the right way even though it feels like it.

Realize that Satan sinned before he ever began recruiting others to join his rebellion. He sinned when he embraced this new path mentally. The Devil unleashed his horrible idea on the world through recruiting other angels and corrupting Adam and Eve. It was sin when he mentally agreed to go along with the idea. There may be things that you have embraced mentally that you need to repent of and seek the Lord's forgiveness. You haven't acted on the idea yet, but you have embraced it mentally. Confession for us is possible and the forgiveness of God waits in the death of the Savior for us to agree with God that the way we are thinking is wrong.

The Five "I wills" of Satan

The next set of scriptures I refer to as the "I wills" of Satan. They mark a level of discontentment that birthed evil when the Devil should have been supremely delighted with all that he had been given. It is possible to be in exactly the right place, doing exactly the right thing, and yet talk yourself into how miserable you are. When we become self-focused, we become like the Devil as he grew his imaginary discontentment into evil.

I will ascend to heaven

As Lucifer, the Devil was already walking in the midst of the stones of fire. He already went onto the mountain of God on a regular basis. But it wasn't enough for him. The special equipment and exalted position became commonplace for him. And instead of dwelling in the most exalted position in the universe in marvelous contentment, his mind suggested that he could climb one more rung higher. Understand that the birth of evil began as a lack of contentment - an innate unease with what God had provided. It was not a desire to maximize oneself. It was a desire to escape the confines of God's rules and God's place. He was the most powerful creature and yet he gave birth to evil through wanting what he could never have -- God's place. Understand that even if he could have succeeded in obtaining God's place, he could not have accomplished what God does. God's place is too much for anyone other than God. Since the Devil fell for this stupid idea when there was no sin, he knew that others would fall for it, too. He has been pitching this same "Be Your Own God" nonsense since he fell for it. When your ambition can never get enough, it becomes evil. At some point you must embrace who you are, what you were made to do, and the relationships you were meant to have. This is called contentment.

Now, let's take a look at what the Devil was specifically saying. In this verse he is referring to the heaven where God dwells. Lucifer did not live there, but he did have access to this dimension. In Scripture it is called the third heaven (2 Corinthians 12:2-4). God dwells in eternity, which is outside of our space-time continuum. The angels dwell in dimensionalities still within our universe and can access eternity with God's permission, but they do not live there. Lucifer embraces the idea that he can live in eternity where God dwells and not just visit there. When he embraced this idea as his destiny, he gave birth to evil. The clawing, the power plays, the corruption, the oppression of others, the tyranny, the megalomania—it all came out of this one mental decision.

I will raise my throne above the stars of God

The "stars of God" is a reference to the angels in the Old Testament. What is tragic about this thought is that he already had an exalted position over the angels, but it was not a throne. It was a servant's towel. He served them as the reflector of the wonder of God. He served them by taking the praise they offered to God into the presence of God. But being in the exalted servant's position was not enough for Lucifer. He saw himself as sitting on a throne above the angels where they served him and where they constantly acknowledged his power, his beauty, his wisdom, and his control. There is something about the need for a throne that has plagued mankind ever since this fateful mental decision. This "I need to be shown to be in charge" is an infection in humanity that whispers constantly to us just like the desire to be free from God's limitations. We must recognize it and reject its siren song.

I will sit on the mount of assembly in the recesses of the north

This is describing a reference to permanence in a place where Lucifer only has temporary access. He wants to sit permanently in a place where he is only temporarily allowed. Just as the high priest was only allowed access to the Holy of Holies once a year on the day of atonement -- and then only to pour the blood of the sacrifice on the mercy seat -- he was not allowed to linger there watching all that happened. He was to do his job and get back out. This was probably the same for Lucifer in his position of anointed cherub who covered. He served God and he served the angels. He walked in the midst of the stones of fire (the magnificent attributes of God) and was on the mountain of God (the dimensionality where God dwells), but he did not get to stay there. His job was to go into this amazing dimension and he wanted to stay there. The mental thought is one of permanence: "I shouldn't just be coming in here occasionally; I should be in here all the time." It may have even started as a wonder at the dimensionality called the mountain of God, but it grew into a desire to plant himself in the midst of the activity of God.

Some have also suggested that this may have referred to the Mount of Messianic authority that was coming. He was, after all, the go-between for God and the angels. Some theologians have taken from this that Lucifer became aware of a much greater go-between for God and humans - God's only begotten Son who would sit on the mount of the assembly. In fact Milton, in his epic poem, *Paradise Lost*, suggests that Lucifer's understanding of God's plan to save mankind after their sin, but not the angels, led him to rebel. It is possible that he wanted to be the only Messiah, the only one between creature and Creator. Again, this would be a growing pride that would eventually consume him.

I will ascend above the heights of the clouds

This may be a reference to angels and any other ascended being as the clouds (Matthew 24:30, 31). Humans are referred to as a part of the clouds that surround Christ at his second coming (1 Thessalonians 4:13-18; Revelation 19:1-16; 2 Thessalonians 1:6-10). This, then, would make it a reference to his desire to officially rule over the invisible realms and all those who dwell in them. Lucifer has a desire to be in charge. His imagination knows no boundaries, and he just keeps pushing for power and independence from the true God.

It is also possible that the clouds refer to the Shekinah glory of God (2 Chronicles 7:1-3). In this case, Satan is thinking he will have more glory or superior glory to the glory of the Almighty. He seems to be drunk with glory. It was not enough to get and receive more than any other creature. He wanted more than any other being. This would mean that Lucifer, who was able to push into the glory of God as he performed his special functions of worship and ministry in God's presence, became at some point enamored with having glory cover his movements, also. But he specifically wants to have more glory than what God exhibits. He wants more. It is also possible that he is saying he wants to push into the secret things of God further than he has in the past and be above the glory of God.

I will make myself like the Most High

This is the final element of his self-deception. He wants the power, majesty, and place of God Almighty. He wants to be worshiped. This seems to be why he creates endless new religions so he can receive praise, worship, and thanks from new angels and different deceived individuals. Mentally he has finished out his rebellion from God. It is these completed and embraced thoughts that led to his expulsion from his exalted position. He has been judged and will be judged further in the future.

What seems to have escaped his notice, however, is that he does not have the inexhaustible essence, nature, or attributes of the Almighty God. He is self-deluded, thinking that because he accesses eternity where God dwells, he is able to *be* God. But he is a creature. He is dependent and does not possess life itself. Now that he has received some of his judgment, he seems to understand this (he has been thrown out of the third heaven and confined to the second and first heavens), but he is still harboring rebellion and is still plotting his eventual overthrow of God. He is no longer the anointed cherub who covers and seems to have been assigned a new position in God's economy -- something like that of a garbage collector. He and those he recruited are involved in bringing consequences to those who sin. Every time we see God wanting to punish a person through a deceptive spirit, one of Lucifer's crew steps up (Judges 9:23; 1 Samuel 16:14-16; 18:10; 1 Kings 22:19-22; 2 Thessalonians 2:11). They are also the spiritual group that God allows to test people to see if they will resist temptation or add to the moral filth and sin in the world (Matthew 12:25-29).

Again it is time to transition to putting these truths into action. How does God want me to avoid my own I-will statements? What level of contentment have I achieved in this life? Please work through these exercises.

Spiritual Exercises

Examine your level of contentment

What strikes you about the five "I wills" of Satan? Like the Devil, have you become self-focused, growing an imaginary discontentment with your circumstances? If it is all about you, then you are not thinking clearly. God's plan involves more than just your happiness. Are you in a self-focused, negative feedback loop? In order to really win, God has to win, other people have to win, and you have to win.

Can you see your situation from beyond your own perspective? What would others say about your life and situation? What would a wise person tell you? Go and see a wise person you know and lay out your case. What do you think would have happened if the Devil had asked to talk with God about what he was thinking before he had committed to it? It is pretty clear that God could have talked him out of the course of thinking that he was going down. I regularly see people who need to talk and listen to wise people about their situation. Too often the people I see come to my office because they want me to tell them they are right. I have to tell them, on most occasions, that they are not being wise -- that they are in a self-focused loop that will lead to their destruction. Get some advice from people who can tell you that you are not seeing things clearly.

List ten things that are right about your life

1.
2.
3.
4.
5.

Where is God blessing you?

1.
2.
3.
4.
5.

How is your level of contentment?

On a scale of 1-10 (1 = not content, 10 = very content), how contented are you with your life? Put a number by each one of these areas. Is this area full of love, joy, and peace? Is this area in need of significant work?

God: 1 2 3 4 5 6 7 8 9 10

Self: 1 2 3 4 5 6 7 8 9 10

Marriage: 1 2 3 4 5 6 7 8 9 10

Family: 1 2 3 4 5 6 7 8 9 10

Work: 1 2 3 4 5 6 7 8 9 10

Church: 1 2 3 4 5 6 7 8 9 10

Finances: 1 2 3 4 5 6 7 8 9 10

Society: 1 2 3 4 5 6 7 8 9 10

Friends: 1 2 3 4 5 6 7 8 9 10

Enemies: 1 2 3 4 5 6 7 8 9 10

God does not want us to be content with immorality, injustice, and hatred. But He does want us to be content in the circumstances that are beyond our control.

The Devil did not embrace a holy contentment as he gave birth to sin. He talked himself into foolishly wanting something more than the incredibly exalted position that God had supplied. Has God placed you in a good place but you have begun to whine, complain, or grouse because it isn't something that you imagined would be better?

Do you have an overflowing amount of love in each of the ten relationships? If you don't, then it is a holy discontent to build up the amount of real righteous love in that relationship.

God:

Self:

Marriage:

Family:

Work:

Church:

Finances:

Society:

Friends:

Enemies:

Is there injustice in any of the ten major relationships of your life? Look at making a difference in those arenas.

God:

Self:

Marriage:

Family:

Work:

Church:

Finances:

Society:

Friends:

Enemies:

An Encounter with God

One of the consistent cures for selfishness and evil is a true encounter with God. Throughout the Scriptures it is an encounter with God that most often recalibrates people so they get over themselves. I think of Abraham, Moses, Joshua, Samuel, Gideon, David, Solomon, Jeremiah, Isaiah, and Ezekiel in the Old Testament. In the New Testament I think of Joseph, Nathaniel, Peter, Paul, the Centurion, the Philippian jailer, John, and Sergius Paulus. This is what we pray for in most people's lives. We want our friend or loved one to have a real-life encounter with God so that it will change them, humble them, and recalibrate their self-focus.

What is amazing about this case where sin, evil, and selfishness started is that the Devil was in the presence of God. But it made no difference. I am intrigued that while most people who have an encounter with God are changed and humbled to the place where they do not generate selfishness anymore. For some it is the opposite. In this case, and a number of other ones in Scripture, some who encounter God are strengthened in their resistance and rebellion: Cain, Lamech, Pharaoh, Korah, Saul, Judas, and Demas. Ironically, the birthplace of evil came into being even though the Devil had access to God in ways that we can only imagine. But he obviously did not have the type of an encounter with God that put his life and world in the right perspective.

Spiritual Exercises

Don't throw it all away

The Devil will encourage you to throw away something that is really good in your life over an imaginary flaw. This is what happened to him, so he knows that it is possible for even very smart people to cast something really good out of their life for a very petty or even an imaginary reason. It could be a marriage that you throw away over a mistake you made. It could be a business you throw away because of tension with a partner or government agency. It could be a friend you throw away because they are not being exactly like you want them to be. It could be a family member that you throw away because they just aren't going along with the program you proposed, or you could throw away the whole family because you think it is too confining. When these impulses to throw the good things in life away persist, *Resist the Devil and he will flee from you.* Hang on to the good gifts that God has given you and do not trample on his grace.

I cannot tell you how many people I have talked with who threw away some of the most precious things in their lives only to realize the huge mistake they made after they had discarded it. I hear things like:

"I should have worked harder in my first marriage."

"My parents weren't bad people; I was just a jerk."

"My kids were the best, but I needed to climb some stupid corporate ladder."

"I miss my old job, but I got mouthy with my boss and threw that life away."

"I had a really close friend, but I really hurt them over something dumb. I really miss them."

Is there something that is really good in your life that you are tempted to throw away?

5

Evil Invades the Human Race
Genesis 3:1-7

We have learned how evil came to be in our universe. It was birthed in the mind of the highest-ranking angel ever created which then spread to other angels. We have learned how he has been judged in the past, is being judged now, and will be judged in the future. Now it is time to examine how he infected the human race. We will find that answer in Genesis 3:1-7.

> *Now the serpent was more crafty than any beast of the field which the LORD God had made. And he said to the woman, "Indeed, has God said, 'You shall not eat from any tree of the garden'?" The woman said to the serpent, "From the fruit of the trees of the garden we may eat; but from the fruit of the tree which is in the middle of the garden, God has said, 'You shall not eat from it or touch it, or you will die.'" The serpent said to the woman, "You surely will not die! For God knows that in the day you eat from it your eyes will be opened, and you will be like God, knowing good and evil." When the woman saw that the tree was good for*

food, and that it was a delight to the eyes, and that the tree was desirable to make one wise, she took from its fruit and ate; and she gave also to her husband with her, and he ate. Then the eyes of both of them were opened, and they knew that they were naked; and they sewed fig leaves together and made themselves loin coverings.

In this passage, the Devil is disguised as a serpent. He injects his own temptations into the human race so that they fall from their state of grace. This famous passage declares how sin entered into mankind as a whole. Sin is not a necessary result of the material world, but rather a result of the selfishness of one woman and one man. The serpent was able to deceive the woman into believing that God was withholding a good thing from her and her husband. He got her to believe that if she partook of the fruit, she would become like God. In one sense, what Satan said is true. If they ate of the tree of the knowledge of good and evil, they would be like God in that they would know good and evil. However, they would not be equal to God. They would be running their lives but without the tools, wisdom, or power to give direction to their lives like God was giving them. Satan remains consistent with his deceptive stratagems since his first temptation. He fell for the idea of being his own god, and he suggests the same thing to others. He focuses people's attention on that which is beautiful and questions why God has not allowed it. He suggests that the desired thing is good and will be helpful. He makes promises that are not true. He suggests that if we commit a particular sin, we will be masters of our own fate. If the believer can see the stratagem of Satan and how he is still using this same methodology, then the believer can be alert and resist the logic of the Devil.

Let's look at these verses one by one to get a better understanding of how sin entered the human race.

Now the serpent was more crafty than any beast of the field which the LORD God had made

Satan uses an animal, called in Hebrew, "nahas" (serpent, viper, something hunted), to inject the same thoughts that derailed his service to God into humanity; thoughts like: You can be your own God; You don't need God, and the like. We don't know what a nahas looked like at this stage of the history of our world. We do know that the nahas was a beast of the field and that it was more *arum* (crafty, cunning) than any other beast of the field. It seems possible from what we learn later (Genesis 3:14) that a nahas was more like a typical four-legged animal in the wild. But after it participated in the deception and corruption of Adam and Eve, it was judged and grounded just like Lucifer eons earlier, becoming a snake/serpent that slithers on its belly. Now Lucifer needs to use a bodily form that will not startle or alarm Adam and Eve. He does not seem to be able to approach Adam and Eve directly in angelic form, so he encases himself in a serpent. We have no record that Adam and Eve ever spoke or interacted with the angels even though they may have been aware of them. (Genesis 3:24)

It does seem strange to us that an animal could communicate with Adam and Eve in the garden. It is clear that Eve and the nahas carried on quite a lengthy interaction.

It may be that the serpent actually talked to Adam and Eve, but it is also possible that the Devil, working from inside of the serpent, projected his thoughts into the minds of Adam and Eve. In this way they were communicating back and forth in some form of mental telepathy. This would clearly have been the way that God and Adam and Eve communicated as they would not have a form to talk with or a mouth to see moving when they talked with God. They would have been used to this mental telepathy form of communication. As a corollary, most scholars feel that the Devil did not appear in a physical form to tempt Jesus in Matthew 4 but that he spoke into Jesus's mind and Jesus in turn spoke back mentally. It is entirely possible that the "crafty" nahas was positioned behind a bush or partially obscured behind a tree where Eve would have known that it was present, but she could not see that it was not actually talking. If this form of communication was common between Adam and Eve and God, then it would not have seemed strange to have this same form of communication with an animal in the garden.

By the way, this is how the Devil tempts us… he drops a thought in our mind and sees if we will go with it. Sort of like a baited fishhook. Do we bite or do we ignore it and move on to other things? We don't have to have a physical person talking in front of us to be tempted. The temptation can come through our mind without anything being said audibly.

And he said to the woman, "Indeed, has God said, 'You shall not eat from any tree of the garden?'"

Eve is standing near the nahas creature maybe not even realizing that this beast is near her. But it speaks to her (either audibly or to her mind). This is a very interesting opening line. It is a negative cast to a positive idea. Instead of saying to her: "Isn't it great that God has allowed you to eat from any tree of the garden you want?" he puts the emphasis on what can't be done. Notice that the Devil does not come out with the real question right away (Don't you want to be your own god?). This questioning of authority and the commands of authority is a favorite with the Devil. It's his method -- "Let me put this perfectly reasonable command in a bad light."

The woman said to the serpent, "From the fruit of the trees of the garden we may eat; but from the fruit of the tree which is in the middle of the garden, God has said, 'You shall not eat from it or touch it, or you will die.' "

Through the nahas creature the Devil is probing Eve's orientation to the rules of God. To her credit she repeated God's orientation to the command about the tree of life. "We can eat from all the fruit trees in the garden," she says. "But there is something different about the fruit tree in the middle of the garden." She almost sees this tree in the middle as not a part of the garden. It is separate. She really was right about this tree. It was separate from the other trees. It had special significance and special consequences. Notice that there was no suspicion in Eve. She never said, "Why are you asking?" She is naïve about the plot that was being hatched against her.

The Devil found in her statement a flaw he was hoping would be there. She embellished the command. God did not say anything about touching the fruit. Look at what God actually said in Genesis 2:8, 9, 15-17.

> *The LORD God planted a garden toward the east, in Eden; and there He placed the man whom He had formed. Out of the ground the LORD God caused to grow every tree that is pleasing to the sight and good for food; the tree of life also in the midst of the garden, and the tree of the knowledge of good and evil.*
>
> *Then the LORD God took the man and put him into the garden of Eden to cultivate it and keep it. The LORD God commanded the man, saying, <u>"From any tree of the garden you may eat freely; but from the tree of the knowledge of good and evil you shall not eat, for in the day that you eat from it you will surely die."</u>*

We don't know whether at this point the nahas creature reaches out to touch the fruit to prove that Eve won't die or not, but it is clear that the Devil goes after the idea of death being tied to this tree. There is the clear suggestion in the text that Eve was close enough to focus on the fruit of the tree. This would suggest that she was close enough to touch it right then.

The serpent said to the woman, "You surely will not die!"

The Devil shocks Eve with his bold contradiction of God's command. He directly attacks the words of God. Now remember that at this point in Eve's life she probably has no idea what death actually is. She may not have seen it among the animals and has clearly not seen it with herself or Adam. She is having a philosophical and ethical discussion with a very sly and evil being about a topic she does not know well. Let this be a lesson. If you are having a discussion about something you are not well versed upon, don't try and defend God's position or you will get completely spun around by the critic of God.

"For God knows that in the day you eat from it your eyes will be opened and you will be like God, knowing good and evil."

The Devil goes on with his attack against God's command. He tells her that what God calls death is really life like she has never experienced it before. He tells her that her eyes will be opened not shut. Isn't the Devil still telling people that what God says is destructive is the pleasure that you really long for? He doesn't tell about the longer-term consequences of the decision, however. He wants to focus the person on the immediate joy, the immediate pleasure. This is always the wrong place to focus. This is the point where everyone who battles with temptation loses. They keep their focus on the immediate gains, ignoring the long-term problems.

When the woman saw that the tree was good for food, and that it was a delight to the eyes, and that the tree was desirable to make one wise.

Notice what the text says that Eve kept looking at: the tree in the middle of the garden. It would seem clear that they were standing near the tree so that in an impulsive action Eve could be close enough to act. Again, through the nahas creature, the Devil has been waiting for Eve to get this close to the forbidden tree. If he is going to get Eve to fall, it will be an impulsive decision and so he must wait until she is close to the tree to have the conversation. Eve lost this crucial battle because her focus remained on the thing that was tempting her. If you and I are going to win our battles with addiction, greed, lust, pride, jealousy, laziness, etc., then we are going to have to focus somewhere else and not on how nice it will be to have what we are being tempted by.

She took from its fruit and ate; and she gave also to her husband with her, and he ate

This is the crucial statement of the entrance of evil into the human race. There are not many statements with as much poignant meaning as this one. Evil, corruption, and selfishness began in the human race right here. It was the point when Eve became more self-focused and less God-focused. She was more interested in making sure that she did not miss something than whether God was pleased with her actions. She knew what God would be pleased with, and yet her own self-focused desires became more important. After all, maybe God used the ominous word *death* as a way of scaring her from what would be a great delight and a great step forward in her development!

Notice the progression in this verse. First, she took (touched) or picked some of its fruit. Nothing changed for her. So her embellishment of the command of God had tricked her. She put up a guardrail to keep her from eating the fruit (don't touch it), and she had invested great significance with keeping that rule of not touching it. But nothing happened when she did touch it. How often I have seen Christian people put reasonable precautionary boundaries around a sin that they feel drawn to so that they do not go all the way to sin. But sometimes they forget to remind themselves or their children that the guardrail itself is not sin. You have not sinned until you actually commit the sin.

Second, she ate the fruit. Some passages suggest that because she was so deceived by the Devil that at this point she was not even sinning because she did not know what she was doing. The text doesn't record any spiritual death when she ate the fruit. Some have suggested that because she was so deceived that it was not until Adam ate that the spiritual death kicked in (because he knew exactly what he was doing). Adam was not deceived and he was clearly choosing to be with Eve over God. He was clearly choosing to be his own god and violate what God had said. The human race fell because of what Adam did, not what Eve did (2 Timothy 2:12-15; Genesis 3:16; 2 Corinthians 11:13).

The third action of Eve is that she does not stop with her own eating of the fruit; she gives some to her husband, Adam. He could see that there was nothing happening when he touched the fruit. Interestingly enough, Adam could have stopped at this point and not eaten the fruit. It was his open and knowledgeable rebellion that plunged the human race out of favor with God. He could have chosen differently. We don't know what would have happened if Adam had obeyed God and turned toward God instead of away from him. We know that whatever that possibility would have looked like for Adam and for Eve, God had all the details of that world worked out also.

The fourth action in the verse and the first action of Adam is the one that condemns the human race and sets us on the rebellious path. Spiritual death engulfs us and we are cut off from the wonder of fellowship with our Heavenly

Father, who perfectly provided for us and anticipated our needs before we were even aware of them. We were shut out of our access to the spiritual dimensions that seemed to have been our privilege in the garden. We were thrown out of the garden and disconnected from God. The garden was not just a garden in a world of jungle; it seems to be a portal where eternity and the physical world could be perceived.

ptop *Then the eyes of both of them were opened, and they knew that they were naked*

There is a lot of wild conjecture about what having their eyes opened actually meant, but it was not good. It was a diminishment of abilities, not an enhancement. Some have suggested that before the fall Adam and Eve saw every creature surrounded in light. We are told that even now, if our eyes were tuned to pick up broader frequencies of light, we would not see the people or animals specifically but instead a much broader aura that surrounds the person which could give a reading about emotions, mental states, and spiritual well-being (the soul). If this were the case then Adam and Eve had never really seen each other in the sense that we look at people today. They saw the light that emanates from their souls. Having one's eyes opened would put the focus on the physical person but hide the view of the soul of the person. This would be a huge change, then, to see just the physical shell that was holding the soul instead of the soul itself. This would also suggest an explanation of why Eve didn't find it odd that an animal talked because she was not used to seeing sound come out of a mouth. It would also give an explanation of why the Devil had to disguise himself in and through a nahas creature rather than coming and interacting with her directly. Exactly what the Devil said would happen happened—their eyes were opened. But having their eyes opened was not good. They were stripped of the spiritual sight and spiritual protection they had previously enjoyed.

As always, the Devil lied about what would happen after Adam and Eve sinned. He made it sound and feel like having your eyes opened was a great thing, but it was a diminishment. It was a guilty thing. It was full of sorrow and broken relationships. When the Devil convinces a man to cheat on his wife by playing up the pleasure of the sexual tryst, he never tells the man about the guilt, the brokenness, the loss of financial security, the relational damage, and the shame that the man will feel afterwards. The Devil puts all the focus on the pleasure and calls it a good thing when it is actually a horrible thing that will deeply damage the man.

And they sewed fig leaves together and made themselves loin coverings

Because Adam and Eve now saw each other only physically, they knew they were naked and needed to cover their bare, physical bodies. The focus was not supposed to be on human, physical bodies. The focus was meant to be on the soul of the person. But, unfortunately, Adam and Eve changed all that with their decision to become self-focused, reaching for power, pleasures, and experiences that God had restricted.

I would be remiss if I did not at least refer to the judgment of God upon the serpent as it has huge implications for our lives. In Genesis 3:14,15 we read:

> *The LORD God said to the serpent, "Because you have done this, cursed are you more than all cattle, And more than every beast of the field; on your belly you will go, and dust you will eat all the days of your life; and I will put enmity between you and the woman, and between your seed and her seed; He shall bruise you on the head, and you shall bruise him on the heel."*

The first part of the judgment is on the nahas creature, specifically. But the last part of God's judgment is on the creature behind the serpent: the Devil. God says, "I will put enmity between you and the woman, and between your seed and her seed. He shall bruise you on the head and you shall bruise him on the heel." Remember, the Devil's job in the past involved angels and universal administration, not humans. Now God has set the Devil and mankind in a struggle. God has assigned and restricted the Devil and his demonic followers to a struggle with humanity. What is this struggle, this enmity? The Devil is not God's enemy—he is our enemy. Imagine how great a comedown it must have been to the Devil that he now must spend all his time administrating tests to humans! He was regal. He was magnificent. He was interacting on the highest levels and because of his sin, he has been assigned to find and take out the garbage of mankind. The Devil is the tester of humans. Humanity is to depend upon God, just as Jesus did in his earthly life, and fight off the temptations (tests) of the Devil. Humans are created for a purpose. (Ephesians 2:10) The Devil tests humans to see if they will stay on course to fulfill that purpose or deviate off course into selfishness and sin.

One could almost think of the Devil as looking over a long assembly line of widgets and his job is to disqualify all those who do not meet specific standards. He, or one of his assistants, tests each one and disqualifies those who do not pass the tests. The good news is that although all have been disqualified for heaven in our own righteousness, God redeems our lives and qualifies us through faith. God gives us a righteousness that we do not qualify to receive. God's way of escape from the disqualifying tests of the Devil is Jesus the Christ, who died and gave himself for us. The Devil takes great delight in disqualifying humans, but God takes greater delight in rescuing those who have been disqualified. Jump into the arms of the Savior who came to earth to rescue you from this struggle with the Devil (that you are losing, by the way). Jesus the Christ will equip you to fight the good fight so you can receive your reward in heaven from God the Father.

What is God looking for from the redeemed? He is looking for faith, righteousness, and love. He knows that it will require complete dependence on Him. He knows that at times we will fail the Devil's tests. He knows how to set us back on our feet and have us fulfill our purpose.

Imagine the disgust of the Devil that those who he has disqualified are being re-qualified through a loophole. The Devil, who was once exalted and powerful, is now a quality control officer whose results are overturned by the owner of the company's gracious and merciful hand. At every turn God foils the Devil. He did not obtain his dreams of being like God. He did not achieve more power and more privilege through his rebellion. He was demoted, restricted, and forced to use his own rebellious nature to serve God. His contribution is regularly overturned and his desires celebrated when ignored or resisted. He is a loser and will lose even more when history has run its course.

Again it is time to transition to doing the Bible from merely studying it. How can this be applied to life? What does God want me to know? What does God want me to feel because of this information? Work through the next few exercises and let the Scripture soak into your life.

Spiritual Exercise

Are you becoming your own god in any area of life?

The Devil sought to convince Adam and Eve that they could become their own gods. They believed him and took action in that direction, thereby introducing evil into this good world that God created.

Is the Devil convincing you to strike out on your own in some area without God?

Where is the Devil trying to get you to become your own god?

Spirituality

Personal Development

Marriage

Family

Work

Church

Finances

Friends

Enemies

The Devil will try and convince you that you could come up with a better plan than God's plan in this area. He will try and convince you that you have grown beyond God's ways of living. It is important to pay attention to the areas where the Devil is whispering to you to strike out on your own and abandon God's ideas.

The consequences of following the temptations of the Devil are always destruction, death, and alienation. But we all have gotten on this train from one time or another. We have said things we shouldn't have, we have done things we wish we could undo, we have embraced emotions way too long and way too deep, we have expressed attitudes that have damaged others, and we have allowed our motives to be evil instead of loving. If you are on this train right now, get off. Begin following the impulses of righteousness.

The battle for the life that you want is not against flesh and blood but against powers and principalities and wicked spirits even in the heavenly places. Do not settle for the failure that the Devil is trying to make you. Even if you have failed in major ways (and you are reading this in prison or alone or unemployed or hung over or bankrupt), accept the grace of God and move forward to claim the life, the purpose, and the accomplishments of God's plan.

6

What Is Satan's Job Now?
Job 1:1-12

One question that comes to our minds when we understand that Satan has been restricted from heaven is: "What is Lucifer doing now since he is no longer the anointed cherub who covers?" We know that as part of his judgment, he has been restricted from the access into the presence of God that he once enjoyed. But has he set up a rebel kingdom somewhere in the invisible universe with God looking for him but not yet able to find him? No. God is sovereign and even the Devil in his rebellion against God is still under his overarching sovereignty.

The Tempter/Tester

Satan expresses himself in a number of ways in his exile on this planet. Each of these expressions of his corrupted self takes place within the confines of God's rules, laws, and assignments. He is truly trying to corrupt, destroy, and devour. You cannot pass the tests of the Devil without the Lord Jesus Christ and the weapons of righteousness that He gives. But you can resist the Devil and pass his tests with the

Lord Jesus Christ. Look at the list of his titles which is a way of telling us what he does:

Tempter	Matthew 4; 1 Thess. 3:5
Lord of the Flies	Matthew 12:24
Satan	Job 1
The Devil	1 Peter 5:8
Roaring Lion	1 Peter 5:8
Belial	2 Corinthians 6:15
Deceiver	Revelation 12:9
Father of Lies	John 8:44
Murderer	John 8:44
Sinner	1 John 3:8
Enemy	Matthew 13:39
Evil One	Matthew 13:39
Angel of Light	2 Corinthians 11:13
God of the World	2 Corinthians 4:4
The Dragon	Revelation 13
The Snake	Genesis 3
Prince of the Power of the Air	Ephesians 2
Ruler of this World	John 17
The Wicked One	Matthew 13:19; Eph. 6:16

What Is Satan's Job Now?

These names reveal something about who he is and what he wants to do to humans. The one role that encompasses all of these schemes is that of tempter or tester. In the various places where the word *tempter* appears in the New Testament, it is the word *peirazo* or *peirasmos* which is "test, tempt, trial" (Matthew 4:3; 1 Thessalonians 3:5; 1 Corinthians 10:13; 2 Peter 2:9). It is the context and the intent that determines what it is. Look at 2 Peter 2:9 to see both failure and success as well as deliverance and punishment -- all as a part of the one process: *The Lord knows how to rescue the godly from temptation, and to keep the unrighteous under punishment for the day of judgment.*

Tempter/Tester is the one summation title that explains what the Devil is and does in his exiled time interacting with humanity. If the Devil and the demons are viewed from the perspective of what they are trying to do to humans, then he can rightly be called enemy, wicked one, murderer, and father of lies. But when it is realized that he is still under the sovereignty of Almighty God, then he is seen as the pawn he is -- an administrator of various kinds of tests. The Devil and his fallen angels are openly rooting for our failure, but God is making us stronger and qualifying us for new levels of service and blessing.

One classic example of this is when God the Father and God the Holy Spirit directed Jesus the Christ, the second person of the Trinity, into the wilderness to be tested (tempted) by the Devil. The Messiah must be tested by a real test that was designed by a tester (the Devil) to have the greatest chance of producing failure. Jesus Christ, the second Adam, gloriously succeeded where the first Adam failed (Romans 5:18,19). Jesus was qualified to be our Savior. He passed every test thrown at Him and won the right to heaven as a perfect human. He then gave up His earned right to heaven and voluntarily surrendered His life so that He might offer His righteousness to those who would call upon His name (2 Corinthians 5:18-21).

Another classic example is the story of Job. Let's dig a little deeper in the book of Job to understand Satan's role as Tempter/Tester under the confines of God's sovereignty. Begin by reading through Job 1:1-12 and pay close attention to the information that is revealed about God's sovereignty and Satan's limits. You will need to read slowly, as there is a lot here. Please take the time to underline various words, write questions in the margin, and circle key words as you read.

> *There was a man in the land of Uz whose name was Job; and that man was blameless, upright, fearing God and turning away from evil. Seven sons and three daughters were born to him. His possessions also were 7,000 sheep, 3,000 camels, 500 yoke of oxen, 500 female donkeys, and very many servants; and that man was the greatest of all the men of the east. His sons used to go and hold a feast in the house of each one on his day, and they would send and invite their three sisters to eat and drink with them. When the days of feasting had completed their cycle, Job would send and consecrate them, rising up early in the morning and offering burnt offerings according to the number of them all; for Job said,* **"Perhaps my sons have sinned and cursed God in their hearts." Thus Job did continually.** *Now there was a day when the*

sons of God came to present themselves before the LORD, and Satan also came among them. The LORD said to Satan, "From where do you come?" Then Satan answered the LORD and said, "From roaming about on the earth and walking around on it." **The LORD said to Satan, "Have you considered My servant Job? For there is no one like him on the earth,** *a blameless and upright man, fearing God and turning away from evil." Then Satan answered the LORD, "Does Job fear God for nothing?* **"Have You not made a hedge about him and his house and all that he has, on every side?** *You have blessed the work of his hands, and his possessions have increased in the land. "But put forth Your hand now and touch all that he has; he will surely curse You to Your face."* **Then the LORD said to Satan, "Behold, all that he has is in your power, only do not put forth your hand on him."** *So Satan departed from the presence of the LORD.* (Job 1:1-12)

According to the Scriptures, Satan is restricted to roaming around on the earth and only addresses God when the other angels turn in some kind of report. God suggests that Satan test Job and his family, but Satan complains that he can't get to Job's family because of the protection God has erected around them due to Job's prayers and spiritual work on their behalf. God says that Job is righteous and yet allows, and even encourages, Satan to severely test him by taking all that he has. This is the Devil's role in this episode. He is given by God the room to concoct a test to see if Job will curse God.

God allows Satan to touch or destroy everything that Job owns, but not to touch him physically, emotionally, mentally, or spiritually.

There seems to be some justification for Satan's desire to test Job in that Job's family does not seem to be as upstanding or righteous as he is. The children seem to be partiers and have the potential to curse God even as Job's wife counsels Job to do. Job is clearly concerned about the lives and spiritual dimension of his children, so much so that he labors in prayer, confession, and sacrifice to purify them (v. 5). It seems that Job's prayers and righteousness has protected them, and God has decided that they have had enough time to develop their own spiritual life.

As a side note, we see this same type of dynamic in two places in Scripture where God talks about a coming judgment and each person's individual accountability.

> *Even though these three men, Noah, Daniel and Job were in its midst, by their own righteousness they could only deliver themselves," declares the Lord GOD.* (Ezekiel 14:14)

> *Even though Noah, Daniel, and Job were in its midst, as I live," declares the Lord GOD, "they could not deliver either their son or their daughter. They would deliver only themselves by their righteousness."* (Ezekiel 14:20)

What Is Satan's Job Now?

> *Then the LORD said to me, "Even though Moses and Samuel were to stand before Me, My heart would not be with this people; send them away from My presence and let them go! And it shall be that when they say to you, 'Where should we go?' then you are to tell them, 'Thus says the LORD: "Those destined for death, to death; and those destined for the sword, to the sword; and those destined for famine, to famine; and those destined for captivity, to captivity."'* (Jeremiah 15:1,2)

This says that a judgment is coming and even if Moses, Samuel, Noah, Job, and/or Daniel were praying, they would only be able to save themselves. God has held off the judgment from Job's children because of Job's spiritual life. But clearly his spiritual life had not penetrated into the lives of the children. That would be different with the next set of children that Job would raise.

The Devil and his fallen angels are testers of humans. They corrupted themselves so now God uses them to see if individual humans will give into selfishness or seek God for direction, wisdom, and forgiveness. Why would God do this? God cannot tempt people (James 1:13) and He has nothing evil in Him. But people need to be truly tested if they are to be truly rewarded for passing the tests. God is not requiring the Devil to do anything that he is not eager to do. Job's story is a perfect example of this. God suggests the test. The Devil wants to know how far he can go in his work. God gives him specific limits. Job is severely tested and sifted in every part of his life. He comes out of the experience a changed man with a much deeper capacity and appreciation for God's wisdom, power, and control (Job 42). God was able to remove the corrupted aspects of Job's life through the testing done by Satan. This is Satan's job to use his corrupted nature to tempt, test and try people as far as God will allow him. Satan didn't like the result in Job's case; Satan was hoping for failure. We might ask why doesn't God just eliminate Satan from the equation? We know that God will do this at the end of history as we know it but according to our understanding of the Scriptures, it is not yet time. (Revelation 20:10)

God's Sovereignty

Scripture tells us more about God's sovereign use of the Devil and deceiving spirits. The deceptive, evil, and corrupting spirits are still under God's control. He has judged them in that He has: 1) removed them from their previous places; 2) He has confined them to this planet; 3) He has limited their activities in numerous ways; and 4) He has repurposed their intense desire for sin and wickedness so that it serves his purposes. They tempt, they bring consequences, and they test whom God allows.

Let's take a look at a number of verses that are uncomfortable unless we understand Satan in the light of God's sovereignty: Judges 9:22-25; 1 Samuel 16:14-16; 18:10; 1 Kings 22:19-23; Matthew 4:3; Luke 22:31; Ephesians 4:25-27; 2 Thessalonians 2:11.

> *Now Abimelech ruled over Israel three years.* ***Then God sent an evil spirit between Abimelech and the men of Shechem;*** *and the men of Shechem dealt treacherously with Abimelech, so that the*

What Is Satan's Job Now?

> *violence done to the seventy sons of Jerubbaal might come, and their blood might be laid on Abimelech their brother, who killed them, and on the men of Shechem, who strengthened his hands to kill his brothers. The men of Shechem set men in ambush against him on the tops of the mountains, and they robbed all who might pass by them along the road; and it was told to Abimelech.* Judges 9:22-25

When it says that God sent an evil spirit, it is better understood that God allowed an evil spirit to torment Abimelech and the men of Shechem because they could not let go of their tribal jealousies and bitterness. These men's choices to hate each other eventually brought the consequences of an evil spirit strengthening their hatred and bitterness. The evil spirit was a judgment and a consequence, but he was also there to expand the sinful choices of these men. That is what happened as their own bitterness moved them to give into the temptations of the evil spirit and compound the wrong of which they were already guilty.

> *Now the Spirit of the LORD departed from Saul,* ***and an evil spirit from the LORD terrorized him.*** *Saul's servants then said to him, "Behold now, an evil spirit from God is terrorizing you. Let our lord now command your servants who are before you. Let them seek a man who is a skillful player on the harp; and it shall come about when the evil spirit from God is on you, that he shall play the harp with his hand, and you will be well."*
> 1 Samuel 16:14-16

The cause-and-effect nature of the spirit world is on display in this verse. Saul had enjoyed the presence and guidance of the Spirit of God. But because of his rebellion and pride in repeated episodes of his leadership, God could no longer guide this willful and self-focused man. Saul was sent a spirit that was more in keeping with his consistent choices -- an evil spirit. The evil spirit was a consequence of Saul's own choices. The Scripture says that the evil spirit came from the Lord. This is true in that God set up the rules and consequences whereby sin is punished. The evil spirits want to test, tempt, and torment; and God releases them to do their job if there is no other spiritual work, rules, or weapons being employed to allow Him to hold them back. It comes back to the choices of the individual and, in most cases, the lack of repentance if they make the wrong choice.

> *Now it came about on the next day that **an evil spirit from God came mightily upon Saul,** and he raved in the midst of the house, while David was playing the harp with his hand, as usual; and a spear was in Saul's hand.* 1 Samuel 18:10

We again see Saul suffering under the evil spirit that was attached to him because of the repeated proud, selfish, and rebellious choices that he had made earlier. There was no advice from his counselors that he should repent and seek the Lord for forgiveness. He most likely could not have had his kingdom restored to his children; but he potentially could have been released from the personal torment, testing, and temptation of this spirit. Instead, his own torment was the instrument to train the next king (David) and prepare him for the heavy weight of leadership decisions. Remember that David was brought to the palace to play music to soothe King Saul when he was the most plagued by the evil spirit. This time in the palace allowed David to see how to run a palace and how not to.

> *Micaiah said, "Therefore, hear the word of the LORD. I saw the LORD sitting on His throne, and all the host of heaven standing by Him on His right and on His left. "The LORD said, 'Who will entice Ahab to go up and fall at Ramoth-gilead?' And one said this while another said that. "Then a spirit came forward and stood before the LORD and said, 'I will entice him.'* ***"The LORD said to him, 'How?' And he said, 'I will go out and be a deceiving spirit in the mouth of all his prophets.' Then He said, 'You are to entice him and also prevail. Go and do so.'*** *"Now therefore, behold, the LORD has put a deceiving spirit in the mouth of all these your prophets; and the LORD has proclaimed disaster against you."*
>
> 1 Kings 22:19-23

In this word from an unheralded prophet, Micaiah, we catch a glimpse of heaven that is incredibly revealing. God had come to the end of dealing with Ahab and his sinful, rebellious, and self-focused ways. Ahab deserves a spirit that will tempt him to a war that will lead to his death. God asks the evil spirits for a volunteer to do this assignment and for details about how they plan on carrying out this righteous judgment on wicked king Ahab. One evil spirit tells about its particular idea of how to tempt Ahab though the mouth of his prophets so that he will move in the wrong direction and be judged. God allows that particular evil spirit to get the assignment and even goes to the unusual step of revealing that He knows that this evil spirit's plan will succeed. It is clear from what we know about God that He knows the result of every choice and every action, but He does not usually tell us or even the angels whether what they are planning to do will succeed or not. In this case God tells the evil spirit that He knows that Ahab will fall for the evil spirit's temptation which would lead to his death. It was time for Ahab's evil reign to be over, and the righteous judgment on him was to be carried out through his listening to a twisted, deceiving spirit.

> *Then Jesus was led up by the Spirit into the wilderness to be tempted by the devil. And after He had fasted forty days and forty nights, He then became hungry. And the tempter came and said to Him, "If You are the Son of God, command that these stones become bread."* Matthew 4:1-3

This is an amazing passage that states that God the Holy Spirit sent Jesus into the wilderness to be tempted by the Devil. If God the Father and God the Spirit required that the Tempter test Jesus to see if His choices would be true and righteous, then we can be confident that it is the Devil's job to test (through temptation and other means) the choices of all humans. We do not completely understand why this test or temptation was necessary. Some theologians tell us that it was not possible for the Son of God to fail these tests. Others say that it was possible but would not happen. What is clear from our vantage point is that before Jesus could be qualified as the Savior of humanity, he must face and pass the tests, the temptation, and the schemes of the Devil just like every other human. Jesus passed with flying colors, relying on God the Father and God the Holy Spirit to get Him through these tests just as we must rely upon God the Father, God the Son, and God the Holy Spirit to pass our tests from the Devil. Jesus did not rely on His own deity to pass this test or He would not be the perfect human. He had to pass this test as a man, completely dependent on the Holy Spirit and God the Father. God the Holy Spirit gave Jesus just the right wisdom from the Word of God to combat each of the tests of the Devil.

> *"Simon, Simon, behold,* **Satan has demanded permission to sift you like wheat;** *but I have prayed for you, that your faith may not fail; and you, when once you have turned again, strengthen your brothers."* Luke 22:31

This is one of the most remarkable passages in the New Testament for what it reveals about God's view of the future, the rules of the spirit world, our sins, and Jesus' on-going role in our lives. Jesus addresses Simon Peter about the fact that Peter would deny knowing Jesus during the pressure-packed time of His arrest. Jesus tells Peter that He knows that he will fail the test that was coming. God the Father and God the Holy Spirit let Jesus know that this will happen to Peter. And Jesus lets Peter know. Realize that this is all still future, but it is certain to happen. The Devil, Jesus tells us, demands that he be given the ability to sift Peter like wheat. In other words, there must be consequences for this grievous sin. Satan is seemingly exercising his right to torment a person who does this level or type of sin. This further confirms that there are rules and procedures for various sins. Satan is demanding the right to follow God's rules and procedures in connection with one of Jesus' disciples because he will sin in a great way. Jesus does not dispute that Satan has the right to do this. In fact, Jesus basically tells Peter that it is coming. But Jesus says that He has prayed for Peter that his faith not fail as the sifting is going on. Satan wants to sift Peter and leave only the bad with Peter becoming a useless, depressed, suicidal wreck as happened to Judas. Jesus needed to allow Peter to be sifted because of his sin; but He wanted the self-serving and egotistical person to be removed, leaving only the good person. Jesus also reveals to Peter that after the sifting is over, he was to strengthen his brothers in the faith. He was still the leader, but this next bit would be brutal. Jesus doesn't tell him to choose differently because it was not in Peter at that time to choose differently. He was going to deny Him. But He needed to know that it was not the end of Peter's life or usefulness to God. If Jesus had not prayed for Peter and if Peter had not cooperated with that prayer, the Christian church could have lost both Judas and Peter on the same weekend.

> *Therefore, laying aside falsehood, SPEAK TRUTH EACH ONE of you WITH HIS NEIGHBOR, for we are members of one another. BE ANGRY, AND yet DO NOT SIN; do not let the sun go down on your anger,* **and do not give the devil an opportunity (a place).**
> Ephesians 4:25-27

This is an absolutely crucial Scripture that states clearly what is implied in a number of other Scriptures. When a person gives in to repeated sin, they give the Devil a place in their life or an opportunity to further test them. Our present world has a very cavalier attitude toward sin and its consequences. We believe that there should always be a recovery or medicine to take away the consequences of sin or guilt. But this is not the case. There are spiritual consequences to sin and to some sins in particular. The sin being talked about in this verse is anger, violence, rage, and murder. When this sin is committed and repeated, it provides the Devil a place in their life. There are other sins that also provide the Devil a place in the life of a person (witchcraft, rebellion, sexual sins, bitterness, pride, wickedness [personal gain at the expense or oppression of others], repeated lying, addictions).

> *For this reason* **God will send upon them a deluding influence** *so that they will believe what is false.* 2 Thessalonians 2:11

This verse tells us that in the future people will reject God and push away at truth and His redemption. For that reason He will send them a deluding influence (read demonic spirits) to encourage them to believe what is false. This judgment will be because of the people's collective choices. They choose to move away from truth and liberty and embrace the bondage of the Devil.

Again and again we see the Devil acting in a particular role that follows the choices of people and the rules and procedures of God. He is not the ruler of a rogue kingdom doing what he wants when he wants. He is the being who brings judgment on those who choose selfishness and rebellion. He is the one who tests our desire for righteousness. He is the one who seeks to drag us down into his world of corruption and moral filth.

The Devil wants to wipe us out but is only allowed to test and tempt us to the degree that God lets him. If the Devil and his fallen angels had free reign, they would destroy us. God limits *what* they can do, *who* they can test, and *why* they can test. Satan is true to his newly corrupted nature expressing perfectly his hatred, perversion, rebellion, and sin within God's limitations and rules to accomplish God's purposes and God's glory. God allows all of us, including Satan, to be true to our own chosen nature and then experience the rewards or punishments of our chosen path (Romans 2:5-8). Satan feeds off our rebellion, sin, and evil; it is most likely his only way to strike back at God. In the midst of the Devil's limitations and judgments, we are offered redemption, and Satan and the fallen angels are not.

The Devil and his angels are not a rebel group doing things God does not know about. Notice that Satan demanded the right to test Peter after his denial of Jesus. He had to ask God for permission to do what he really wanted to do. An independent rebel does not ask permission to attack. Satan is not an independent rebel. He is under God's control even though all he wants to do is bring about corruption and evil. Some theologians have called the Devil God's pit bull. Satan wants to test us and leave only the bad. God allows the test to bring brokenness or reveal the good. People have choices to make and if they choose poorly, God sends tests to see if they want to keep going down that road. If they keep choosing sin, selfishness, pride, lust, and rebellion, then the consequences for their poor choices will become increasingly difficult. These consequences may include deceptive spirits and/or deluding influences as well as diseases, enemies, bankruptcy, and prison. Notice what Ephesians 4:26-27 says: *we should avoid falsehood and anger because we do not want to give the Devil a place in our lives.*

This role of Tempter/Tester is the role that the Devil has been assigned by God. His corrupted nature wants humans to fail. God wants the test to be real so that the person can be blessed when they pass. The tests are real. Not every test that God sends into our lives is from the Devil, but some are and we need to pass. We need to choose righteousness and turn away from sin. We need to grow, develop, and learn from the tests that God allows into our lives (James 1:2-4).

Bringing It Home

What does all of this mean for you? How can we use what we learned about the Devil's role on earth today for our benefit? Remember that God was able to remove the "me first" orientation in Peter through the sifting that the Devil did following the denial of Christ. God brought out in Peter the rock-like nature that helped established the church in the early days. God used the thorn in the flesh in the Apostle Paul's life to keep him from exalting himself, which would make him disqualified for service (2 Corinthians 12:1-10). God used the tempting of King David on a number of occasions to bring back out the man who had a tender heart for the Lord (1 Samuel 25; 1 Chronicles 21:1; 2 Samuel 11).

In a sense Satan is in charge of product testing. The Devil and his fallen angels are trying to get humans to fail. God wants them to succeed, but they must choose. Even if a person fails the test it is a chance for a choice. Will they reach out for the mercy of God? God does not choose for people, arbitrarily assigning some people to the good camp and other people to the bad camp. He elevates us to a place where we can choose. He empowers us with faith, with grace, and with mercy; but we must choose (John 3:16; Joshua 24:19-23). Once we have chosen, he protects, keeps, and defends (Matthew 23:37; Philippians 1:6; 1 John 2:2; Jude 24; Romans 8:28-30). Because the Devil corrupted himself through selfishness and pride, God put him in charge of testing others' corruptibility. In this way God ensures that the tests are real and the choices are real.

It is important to note that God has done a unique thing with humans that He did not do with angels. If a human fails under the testing, God provides forgiveness for them in the life, death, and resurrection of His Son, Jesus the Christ. If they will turn to Him in dependence and ask for forgiveness, it is theirs. This opportunity for redemption was not extended to the angels. They are not a race but individual creations of God. God would have had to die for each one to have offered redemption to them. The Scriptures tell us that angels long to look at the wonder of salvation (1 Peter 1:12). It must be amazing to them that humans can rebel, sin, and even walk away from God; and yet God reaches out to us in mercy and grace. And if the humans repent, they can come back to God and will one day be exalted above the angels as trophies of God's love and grace, ruling over the angels (1 Corinthians 6:2,3; Ephesians 1:6; 2:7). From the angels' point of view salvation reveals aspects of the Almighty that are staggering. God's heart of love is without measure and this shows it. It is guaranteed that you will be tested in this world. There will be temptations, emotional distractions, and mental and physical pressures to get you to give up your destiny and to get you to abandon righteousness. God wants you to succeed even as He has commissioned the testing (Matthew 4:3-10). You cannot succeed without the testing and the testing confirms the level of your success.

Be comforted by the fact that there are rules that corrupted angels must follow. They come to test and they will use temptation to test. If you allow pornography in your life long enough, they come to test your commitment to righteous sexuality. If you allow movies and materials full of witchcraft and false religion, they will come to test your embrace of the one true God. If you listen to or speak enough swear words, they will come to test your commitment to emotional control and avoiding verbal abuse to those you love. If you regularly profit from stealing in some form, then they will come to test your commitment to honesty, integrity, and property rights. If you blow up your relationships because of your selfishness, you will be given multiple tests and temptations to where you must give up some form of selfishness in order to retain a relationship (marriage, children, friend, work, God, etc.) The demons' tests are real with real consequences if you fail. God also is ready to bring real blessings and growth if you pass the test.

Jesus tells us in the Lord's Prayer to ask God the Father not to lead us into testing and temptation but to deliver us from the evil one. This is good news in that we can skip some testing through prayer. The Apostle Paul tells us in the Armor of God passage (Ephesians 6:10-18) that prayer is just one of eight weapons that allows us to pass, skip, and/or be protected from the testing (work) of the Devil. The Devil does not have to win; we don't have to fail. To win a righteous life is made available to us in Christ; take advantage of it. The Devil wants to trap us in a hellacious world full of betrayal, sin, and fear. God wants us to turn away from sin, pass the test, be blessed, and glorify Him in the process.

In Summary

Let's sum up some lessons about the Devil, demons, and testing. The picture that emerges from the Scripture is quite different than what we have been led to believe about the Devil. Since the Devil introduced sin into the perfect and morally good universe that God made, the Devil will now constantly be involved in and with sin. He caused sin, therefore, he will be testing it, punishing it, and cleaning it up. Remember, when Lucifer was originally created he was perfect in beauty, perfect in wisdom, and blameless with access to the presence of the Holy God. Now his job is to -- every day, every hour -- be involved with the moral filth he brought into being. He is a tester of righteousness by being a tempter to sin. He gives people choices and they live or die with the consequences of their choices (Galatians 6:7). God will also judge the evil and his followers more completely in the future (Revelation 20).

God allows and at times sends trials, testing, and temptations to come into our lives to strengthen, test, qualify, and bring us to repentance. Sometimes the Devil and the fallen angels who followed him in rebellion administer those trials, tests, and temptations. Not all testing is done by the Devil though. Not all trials come because we have sinned. God has assigned the Devil and his demons new duties in keeping with their selfish, sinful, and rebellious desires. They have chosen to think selfishly, to want sin, and to encourage pride and rebellion; so God has set them up as the ones who test the choices of mankind and bring the consequences when humans choose poorly (Luke 22:31). The battle is for the souls of men and women. What will individual men and women choose? Will they repent after they have chosen badly or will they push deeper into sin? Will they reach out to the merciful God or will they strengthen themselves in their rebellion and pride? These tests are for real. As they come from the Devil, they are designed to make a person fail. As God allows the tests, they are designed to purify, strengthen, and move you more fully into the will of God. There is no testing or temptation that has overcome you that is not common to mankind, and with the testing or temptation, God has provided a way of escape that you may bear it (1 Corinthians 10:13).

Again let's push this into our lives and bring about changes because of the truth that God allows and at times sends the Devil to test and/or tempt us.

Spiritual Exercise

Evaluating tests and trials

God sends and allows tests and trials into our lives, and at times He even allows the Devil to administer those tests and trials. God wants you to grow from the tests. He wants you to pass the tests. If the test is administered by the Devil, he wants you to fail so he can disqualify you from the life God really wants you to have. But that is not God's intent. Even if you have failed in the past -- and everyone has -- focus on God's intent and God's ultimate goal, not the failure.

The following are possible tests that God may be allowing in your life. The Devil may administer some as well as the world, your friends, your government, your loved ones, etc. It can be helpful to think through what kind of test you are going through. The Apostle James says that we should rejoice when various trials crowd into our lives because they come to test our faith. And when they are done, we are left more able and complete for the challenges of life.

1. Does the test seem to be one designed to see if you are ready for a new level of service (kind of like an application)?

2. Does the test seem to be designed to force you to learn new ways of dealing with your problems (kind of like homework at school)?

3. Does the test seem to be designed to force you to realize how dependent upon the Lord you really are and that you do not have this area handled (kind of like re-sizing your ego)?

4. Does the test seem to be one designed to strengthen you for more service in your present situations (kind of like practice and workouts)?

5. Does the test seem to be one designed to make you choose between righteousness and sin (kind of like an enticing temptation)?

6. Does the test seem to be designed to reveal areas of sin that you may have been ignoring (kind of like an audit)?

7. Does the test seem to be one designed to get you to repent from sin you have been committing (kind of like a sting operation)?

Spiritual Exercise

Taking a testing/trial inventory

In what areas are you being tested at present? Is it possible that some of the testing is coming from the Devil and his fallen angels who really do want to see you fail? Let's look at the various relationships of your life and see where the tests are taking place. In each of the areas I have suggested some possibilities, but this is not an exhaustive list. Ask God to show you what is going on in the pressure that we are facing. Many times our tests are the reproofs of life that you are ignoring, and God is sending reinforcing consequences to get us pay attention (Proverbs 1:22).

1. Your spirituality?

    - Is there pressure to doubt God, the Bible, or Christianity?

    - Is there pressure to ignore God?

    - Is there pressure to do something other than pursuing God?

    - Is there a desire to do something God wouldn't approve of, so there is a new amount of doubt about God?

2. Your marriage?

- Is there pressure to argue with your spouse?

- Is there an opportunity to cheat on your spouse?

- Is there pressure to give up on your marriage?

3. Your family?

- Is there pressure to leave your family?

- Is there pressure to be more demanding and selfish?

- Is there pressure to avoid time with your family

- Is there pressure to make your family everything to the exclusion of the rest of life?

- Is there pressure to be involved in a hobby, service, or organization that is more enjoyable than time with family?

4. Your work?

  - Is there pressure to put so much time into work that everything else suffers?

  - Is there pressure to be apathetic at work?

  - Is there pressure to make work your "everything" because it is so enjoyable?

5. Your church?

  - Is there pressure to avoid worship services and serving opportunities?

  - Is there pressure to give too much time to the church so that other areas are not handled well?

  - Is there pressure to complain, gripe, or criticize people at the church?

6. Your finances?

  - Is there pressure to steal or take a shortcut to have more money?

- Is there pressure to make a decision quickly in regards to money?

- Is there pressure to spend money in some direction without real clarity if it is righteous or God's will?

7. Your friends?

   - Is there pressure to accept a new friend who embraces a sinful lifestyle?

   - Is there pressure to do certain things with your friends that your conscience is not feeling right about?

   - Is there pressure to overlook a possible friend because they are different or wounded?

8. Your enemies?

   - Is there pressure to seek vengeance against a person who really wounded you or did evil against you?

   - Is there pressure to hate a person who is opposing you?

- Is there pressure to write a person off who just rubs you the wrong way, but is seeking your help, support, or wisdom?

Conclusion

Let's take a look at what we now know because of this examination of Satan and the origin of evil. As you read each of these summation statements, make a mental note (or one on the page) about whether you need to go back and study that truth in the appropriate chapter.

- We know that God created a good and excellently organized universe which included all kinds of laws, process, and material aspects as well as many types of living organisms (varieties of angels, people, and plant and animal life).

- We know that originally all the angels who were created were good and glorified God.

- We know that one angel was invested with special beauty, special wisdom, and a special suit in order to perform a unique assignment for God. He was designed to go into the direct presence of God and mediate God's presence and attributes out to the other angels as well as mediate the praises of the angels back to God.

- We know that even though this high-ranking angel was specifically designed for his particular job and particularly equipped to accomplish his esteemed role, he became discontented as he imagined a greater role for himself.

- We know that as this high-ranking angel became more and more self-focused, he embraced his imagined new role, and led a rebellion against God to secure his imagined role.

- We know that this high-ranking angel eventually led a third of the other angels into rebellion against God.

- We know that this high-ranking angel (Lucifer) was judged for his actions and severely limited in what he could do and where he could go. He was in some ways confined to this planet. His assignment was changed from a place of incredible privilege to being just a lackey.

- We know that Lucifer and his followers were given new diminished assignments because of their sinfulness and self-focus. They were given the assignment of testing humans and punishing those who failed in their choices. These angels became tempters and delivery agents for some of the consequences to those who failed to make moral choices.

Conclusion

- We know that Lucifer the fallen angel, who led a rebellion against God, was allowed to test Adam and Eve to see if they would stay obedient to God trusting Him for their life and success.

- We know that Adam and Eve gave into the same discontentment and self-focus that spoiled the soul of the Devil. They failed the test and were judged for their failure to live in dependence upon God.

- We know that Adam and Eve's discontentment, self-focus, and decision to be their own god plunged them and all of their offspring into spiritual darkness, cut off from the life that is in God.

- We know that evil began as self-focused discontentment and has now grown into a worldwide phenomenon in which millions of people are damaged and destroyed because of the self-focused choices of mankind and angels.

- We know that evil is doing harm to oneself, others, or society at large. It begins as a self-focused discontentment that grows until the person acts to get what this self-centered impulse has convinced the individual that it must have -- no matter who gets in the way -- or who gets hurt.

- We know that God has given in His Word clear instructions as to when humanity is approaching an evil action. These moral lines are broadly spelled out in the Ten Commandments. An action becomes evil when you win at another's expense.

- We know that an angelic being gave birth to evil, but it does not need angels to continue its existence and spread. Humans can and do embrace their own self-focused discontentment without the help of Satan and his demons.

- We know that evil is parasitic on good. Good can exist by itself but evil cannot. Evil is always a twisting of the good in some way. Evil and good are not dualistic opposites. Evil is a heterodox growth on the good.

- We know that Satan and his demons exist at present to tempt humans to make the wrong choices (like they did), and then bring punishments for the very wrong choices they were trying to induce. This makes the test, temptations, and trials real. The choices are real and the consequences are real.

- We know that the Devil has been partially judged for his rebellion and will be more fully judged in the future. The Devil, and all the evil angels who followed him in rebellion against God's plan, will eventually be placed into a containment field specifically designed to allow none of their self-focused rebellious perspectives and actions to escape back into the new heavens and the new earth. This containment field is called in the Scriptures, the Lake of Fire.

- We know that the Devil's present role in God's Universe is to test those whom God wants tested, and to bring consequences to those who sin like he did. (He has a number of ways to test people called his schemes.)

- We know that God regularly tests people to determine what is in their souls and to send them down the appropriate path in life to match the state of their soul. "God is not mocked, whatsoever a man sows that shall he also reap." (Galatians 6:7) "God will render to each person according to their deeds." (Romans 2:6)

- We know that God does not have the Devil administer all the tests He gives people, but God does have the Devil and his demons administrate some of the tests and trials that come into people's lives.

Spiritual Exercise

Enjoy the wonder of God's creation.

When was the last time you enjoyed the wonder of God's creation? Everyone has some aspect of creation that is life-giving. Too often we allow the busyness of life to take us away from that aspect of creation. Schedule time every week to let the energy and grace of God drip into your life through creation.

Are you allowing discontentment to grow in your heart?

Discontentment is often a function of neglect. If there is a relationship that we have neglected, then it can begin to grow a discontent in our hearts. If we throw ourselves back into the relationship worth preserving by spending time, giving words of affirmation, serving the other person, appreciating the person, etc., then we can re-inflate the relationship. Then the joy, the love, the significance, and the meaning will return. Don't let a relationship slip into discontent; fight for it with your life.

Examine the good things in your life.

When was the last time you made a list of all the good things in your life? Make one now!

Conclusion

Where's your focus?

If we were to talk with the people closest to you, would they say that you are self-centered or focused on God and others? Sit down with someone you trust and allow them to pour out their perspective on this.

Don't throw the good things away.

Are you about to throw away something that is really good but needs work or some tender loving care? Have you thrown away something or someone that was really precious to you in the past? Is it possible to try and reconcile? How can you learn from that past foolishness and be wiser in the present and future?

Where are you sinning?

Can you remember a recent time when you allowed God to comb through your life and point out areas where you have sinned by omission (things you should have done but didn't)? Where you have sinned by commission (things that you shouldn't have done but you did)? Where you have sinned by wickedness (you gained at the expense of other)?

Take some time right now or schedule an hour in the next three days when you will ask God to search you and see if there is any sinful ways in you.

> *Search me, O God, and know my heart: try me, and know my thoughts: and see if there be any wicked way in me, and lead me in the everlasting way.* Psalms 139:23-24

Are you being tested?

Are you being tested right now by the Devil to make an immoral choice? What are you being tempted to do that you shouldn't do, and what should you do instead of what you are being tempted to do?

What do you have to look forward to if you pass this test? It is so much easier to pass the tests when you can picture what rewards, blessings, and joys are on the other side of this difficult period. What are they?

It is not uncommon when our souls are being tested for us to have some awful qualities bubble to the surface. This is the refining process. If awful stuff is showing up, then God is testing. Now is the time to find ways to remove those qualities, reactions, and attitudes from our lives. What is bubbling to the surface in your life that needs to be removed?

Where are you compromising righteousness?

Are you compromising in ways that are really bothering you and doing things you know to be wrong? Are you gaining at other people's expense? Usually this involves lying,

Conclusion

cheating, swearing, rebelling, having sex outside of marriage, stealing, scheming, deception, etc.

If you have identified some areas or relationships where you are gaining at other people's expense and you want to stop, then you have to answer a few questions: When will you stop? How will you stop? How will you restore what you have damaged? How will you keep yourself from going back and doing this again?

Appendix 1
The Disciplines of Repetition
Biblical Meditation

We have done a fairly extensive look at three sections of Scripture, but it is always helpful to meditate on the biblical verses yourself. Therefore I have included this overview of the techniques of biblical meditation and the blank meditation worksheets to allow you to ruminate over these passages yourself. I have included ten blank sheets so that you can try all the various biblical techniques on each passage. I can remember my youth pastor always wanting ten pages of biblical meditation worksheets. He wanted me to press the Scriptures through every part of who I was: my spirit, my mind, my will, my emotions, and even my body. You never know which of the techniques will unlock an insight, a connection to God, a new application.

People are talking about meditation these days as though it were the sole property of the Eastern religions. Eastern religions practice a form of meditation. Using broad general categories, there are two types of meditation: **Emptying forms** of meditation and **content-based forms** of meditation. All meditation is the focused attention of the mind upon something. In emptying forms of meditation the mind is focused on a nonsense idea, word, phrase, or a logical absurdity in order to attempt an escape from the present space-time logical constraints. In content-based meditation the mind is focused on some form of content. There are three forms of content-based meditation: materialistic, spiritual and biblical. Biblical meditation is "content-based" meditation with biblical words, ideas, phrases, and precepts as the meditated content. The new biblical qualities, reactions, and ideas will become a part of the person who is being shaped into Christ-likeness. The goal of the Christian is to have the Lord's thoughts become their thoughts (Isaiah 55:6-8, Psalm 1:1-3; Colossians 3:16; Joshua 1:8; Philippians 4:8; Deuteronomy 6:6-9).

The Incredible Power of Biblical Meditation

The most powerful form of transformational life-change known to man is meditation. In fact, no long-term life-change can take place without this meditation. The tragedy in Christian circles is that this powerful method is often unknown, unused, and in some cases even reviled. Biblical meditation was common practice in the Christian church for 1900 years. Yet in the last 150 years biblical meditation has been left behind in the modern church as it searches for newer programs and crowd-pleasing techniques. The prophet Amos tells of a time when there will be a famine in the land: *Not a famine for bread, or a thirst for water, but rather for hearing the words of the Lord.* (Amos 8:11) We are living out a fulfillment of that vision. More Bibles are printed than ever before and yet the power of the Bible is not connecting with the souls of God's people. All the power people want for transformational life-change is near but remains untapped.

Appendix 1

What is Biblical Meditation?

The idea behind biblical meditation is taken from a sheep or cow chewing its cud. The animal chews the grass and works it into a mush and then swallows it. It then brings it back up later to chew it some more. It repeats this process until all the nutrients have been extracted from the grass. Meditation is murmuring or repeating the concepts, ideas, and words of Scripture to extract all the richness and wisdom.

Biblical meditation is referred to in a number of ways in the Scriptures: delighting in Scripture (Psalm 119:16, 34, 47, 70); delighting in the Lord (Psalm 37:4); letting the Word of God richly dwell in your soul (Colossians 3:16); setting your mind on things above (Colossians 3:1); setting your mind on the Spirit (Romans 8:6); renewing your mind (Romans 12:2).

What Are the Techniques of Biblical Meditation?

Down through the centuries of Judeo-Christian history strong believers have discovered a number of methods for "chewing" Scripture. These techniques move the believer significantly forward in their pursuit of God and attainment of Christ-like living. The following list is not meant to be exhaustive or prioritized. Some will find certain techniques more helpful than others.

Confessionalize Scripture

To confessionalize Scripture is to take the Bible through your will. It is the process of comparing your life with the biblical standard and asking God whether this is true of your life. Every phrase or sentence of Scripture forms a way of examining your life.

First, each truth or action exposed in that Scripture is confessed as true and important. "Dear Lord, I agree with you that Christians should love one another."

Second, each truth or action is confessed as something you are doing or something that you are not doing. "Dear Lord, I freely admit that I am having a very difficult time loving this person right now. I know that I should, but I do not. Create in me a heart of love for this person." Or, "Dear Lord, I am encouraged to say that I am acting in a loving way toward my wife. I thank you for teaching me how to love her." Specifically and openly comparing your life with Scripture is a powerful way to draw the Bible through your will.

Visualize Scripture

The idea of biblical mediation through visualization is to take a passage of Scripture and make it come to life in your mind. It can be referred to as making a mental picture or movie of a biblical scene or concept. For thousands of years all societies have declared the power of the mind to shape behavior and achievement. There are at least two kinds of

Appendix 1

Scripture to visualize: narrative and didactic. **Narrative visualization** is where one sees a biblical story actually taking place. Smelling the smells; hearing the sounds around the event; touching the equipment or clothing of the individuals in the story. In narrative meditation there needs to be focused attention on the biblical detail and an educated imagination to fill out the narrative story line.

The second type of visualization is **didactic visualization**. This is where one pictures the truth of Scripture being lived out in present reality. When this is applied to doctrinal aspects of Scripture, the doctrinal truths are pictured. One might recognize the unseen hand of God moving on, in, and through the men who penned the Scripture to keep it error free and accurate. When this is applied to a practical principle for living, the principle is viewed as being lived out in life, such as being gentle in response to a sarcastic remark as in Proverbs 15:1. The key idea here is to actually picture oneself living out a scriptural concept. What has to be done to get in a position to live this biblical idea? If you can't see yourself doing a righteous idea in your mind, you will never do it. You have to see it before you will do it.

One of the clearest examples of this type of meditation is in Colossians 3:1-14. The apostle orders Christians to "set their minds on the things above;" "Put to death your earthly members: fornication, impurity, etc;" "Put on a heart of compassion, kindness, humility..." Each of these commands is a mental exercise designed to cause you to "see" what is not your present experience. We are to see ourselves enjoying the wonders of heaven, intimacy with God, the qualities of

Christ, entering into the heavenly economy, etc. We are to picture ourselves as unresponsive and unaffected by those temptations that are the most powerful in our lives. We are to make a mental movie of the qualities of Christ being our normal lifestyle. Mental movie-making of biblical ideas is God's way of renewing our minds.

Personalize Scripture

Personalizing Scripture can bring the power of an individual Scripture directly into your emotions. This technique is accomplished by inserting your name or a personal pronoun into a verse when saying it. One of the reasons that the Psalms are such a popular section of the Scripture is that in many cases they are already personalized. Years ago I was counseling a woman who was really having a hard time staying in her marriage. She wanted to end her marriage and pursue her selfish desires. I asked her to pray and ask God what she should do. She began praying and God began to bring back into her mind the Scriptural directions for wives in Ephesians 5 with her name woven through the commands. This was immensely powerful. "God spoke to me," she said. "He spoke to me and I will never forget it." This time of prayerful meditation was a turning point in her life. She went back home and threw herself into her marriage with new hope and determination. Her marriage improved dramatically because God had spoken through Scripture as it was being personalized to her.

Appendix 1

Record Insights

Usually during the time when you are using the other methods of biblical meditation you will become aware of ancillary questions, insights, connections, or bits of wisdom that are in some ways connected to the Scripture but may not be the main points of the passage. These are called insights. It is as though God begins to open the Scriptures to you and the levels of wisdom contained within it. Christians have usually found that if they write down insights as they are meditating, then they receive more of these insights. It is almost like saying to God, "I'm paying attention." Sometimes this is called spiritual journaling. A meditation journal is a helpful way of recording your reactions, thoughts, insights, and promptings during meditation.

Pray Scripture

This technique is to turn the actual phrases of Scripture into prayers. It is very educational to pray God's desires back to Him. As your mind seeks ways to turn various passages into requests you will uncover new angles and depth of understanding on the will of God. In every passage there are many different ways to turn the truths into prayer requests. This type of prayer resembles the Apostle Paul's prayers in Ephesians 1:18-21 and 3:14-21. Asking for scriptural realities is often the best kind of praying for it keeps us from asking from a limited materialistic perspective. When we verbalize what God wants us to desire, we see the stark contrast between God's desires for us and our own fleshly desires.

Harmonize

There are at least two ways to meditate on Scripture through song. One is to sing the actual words of Scripture and adjust the tune to work with the unaltered words of the biblical text. The second method for meditating on Scripture through song is to take the truths, ideas, or concepts of the Scripture and sing those. This is a little easier and more free-flowing. When singing the Scripture it does not matter if it is great music, just that you are expressing the truths, feelings, and desires of Scripture. You will laugh, smile, ponder, and re-commit to the Lord as you sing the words or concepts of Scripture. It is really an enjoyable process, but it takes a little courage to get started.

Open the Bible, pick a tune you know, and begin singing the words of Scripture to the tune. Another way to harmonize the Scripture is to look at a passage or a Christian doctrine and write down three or four truths. Start making up a song about those truths. The tune and the words are changeable as long as they accurately reflect the truth of Scripture. Many of our great hymns and gospel songs have come from just such meditations. The writers were not trying to write great hymns but to express their heart and soul regarding the truths of God. "Amazing Grace" by John Newton, "Amazing Love" by Charles Wesley, and various versions of the Apostles Creed that have been set to music are all examples of this type of meditation.

Appendix 1

What Are the Results of Biblical Meditation?

God makes some amazing promises in the Scripture regarding biblical meditation. In Joshua 1:8 and Psalm 1:1-3 God promises believers if they meditate on His law, they will be prosperous and successful. The mind filled with biblical principles and laws will avoid many of the hidden reefs that sink other people's lives. When a Christian purposefully fills their mind with Scripture, then the God of peace will move in and reassure that person that He is still in charge and He has a way through every storm (Colossians 3:16). In Psalm 119:97-100, God promises believers that they will gain wisdom beyond their years if they meditate upon biblical concepts.

When Are the Best Times to Meditate?

God has specifically suggested particular times to ruminate on Scripture (Deuteronomy 6:6-9; Psalm 1:1-3; 4:4; 63:6). **First**, the Scripture says to meditate when we sit in our homes. This means that one must turn off the TV at times. Many business travelers would lessen the temptations of travel and increase intimacy with God by turning off the television when they travel. **Second**, the Scripture suggests that people should get into the habit of reorienting their minds to Scripture as they are going from place to place. This is a time to pre-plan the next appointment using biblical concepts and qualities. A **third** time to meditate on Scripture is right before going to sleep. As people focus their minds on the concepts, qualities, and words of Scripture right before they drift off to sleep, it allows their subconscious mind to embrace these concepts. A **fourth** time to meditate each day is when the day begins. Many Christians set aside time each morning to spend extended time with God through biblical meditation. A **fifth** time for meditation is the night watches. These are times in the middle of the night spent with God and His Word.

The Disciplines of Repetition: Conclusion

Memorization and meditation are not the only disciplines of repetition, but they have for centuries formed two of the more crucial practices that develop the spiritual Christian. It is not enough merely to understand these practices; one must actually do them on a regular basis to impact the depths of the soul. The goal of memorization and meditation is to give God the Holy Spirit an ever-increasing supply of language and concepts to use when communicating with us.

Appendix 2

Ezekiel 28:12-19 - *Son of man, take up a lamentation over the king of Tyre and say to him, "Thus says the Lord GOD, 'You had the seal of perfection, full of wisdom and perfect in beauty. "You were in Eden, the garden of God; every precious stone was your covering: the ruby, the topaz and the diamond; the beryl, the onyx and the jasper; the lapis lazuli, the turquoise and the emerald; and the gold, the workmanship of your settings and sockets, was in you. On the day that you were created they were prepared. "You were the anointed cherub who covers, and I placed you there. You were on the holy mountain of God; you walked in the midst of the stones of fire. "You were blameless in your ways from the day you were created until unrighteousness was found in you. "By the abundance of your trade you were internally filled with violence, and you sinned; therefore I have cast you as profane from the mountain of God. And I have destroyed you, O covering cherub, from the midst of the stones of fire. "Your heart was lifted up because of your beauty; you corrupted your wisdom by reason of your splendor. I cast you to the ground; I put you before kings, that they may see you. "By the multitude of your iniquities, in the unrighteousness of your trade you profaned your sanctuaries. Therefore I have brought fire from the midst of you; it has consumed you, and I have turned you to ashes on the earth in the eyes of all who see you. "All who know you among the peoples are appalled at you; you have become terrified and you will cease to be forever.' "*

Journal of Biblical Meditation

Scripture	
Slow Repetition	
Memorization	
Study	
Personalize	
Confessing	
Praying	
Envisioning	
Singing	
Journal Insights	
Diagramming/ Analogy	
Personal Translation	

Appendix 2

Journal of Biblical Meditation

Scripture	
Slow Repetition	
Memorization	
Study	
Personalize	
Confessing	
Praying	
Envisioning	
Singing	
Journal Insights	
Diagramming/ Analogy	
Personal Translation	

Journal of Biblical Meditation

Scripture	
Slow Repetition	
Memorization	
Study	
Personalize	
Confessing	
Praying	
Envisioning	
Singing	
Journal Insights	
Diagramming/ Analogy	
Personal Translation	

Appendix 2

Journal of Biblical Meditation

Scripture	
Slow Repetition	
Memorization	
Study	
Personalize	
Confessing	
Praying	
Envisioning	
Singing	
Journal Insights	
Diagramming/ Analogy	
Personal Translation	

Journal of Biblical Meditation

Scripture	
Slow Repetition	
Memorization	
Study	
Personalize	
Confessing	
Praying	
Envisioning	
Singing	
Journal Insights	
Diagramming/ Analogy	
Personal Translation	

Appendix 2

Journal of Biblical Meditation

Scripture	
Slow Repetition	
Memorization	
Study	
Personalize	
Confessing	
Praying	
Envisioning	
Singing	
Journal Insights	
Diagramming/ Analogy	
Personal Translation	

Journal of Biblical Meditation

Scripture	
Slow Repetition	
Memorization	
Study	
Personalize	
Confessing	
Praying	
Envisioning	
Singing	
Journal Insights	
Diagramming/ Analogy	
Personal Translation	

Appendix 3

Isaiah 14:12-14 - *How you have fallen from heaven, O star of the morning, son of the dawn! You have been cut down to the earth, you who have weakened the nations! But you said in your heart, I will ascend to heaven; I will raise my throne above the stars of God, and I will sit on the mount of assembly in the recesses of the north. I will ascend above the heights of the clouds; I will make myself like the Most High.*

Journal of Biblical Meditation

Scripture	
Slow Repetition	
Memorization	
Study	
Personalize	
Confessing	
Praying	
Envisioning	
Singing	
Journal Insights	
Diagramming/ Analogy	
Personal Translation	

Appendix 3

Journal of Biblical Meditation

Scripture	
Slow Repetition	
Memorization	
Study	
Personalize	
Confessing	
Praying	
Envisioning	
Singing	
Journal Insights	
Diagramming/ Analogy	
Personal Translation	

Journal of Biblical Meditation

Scripture	
Slow Repetition	
Memorization	
Study	
Personalize	
Confessing	
Praying	
Envisioning	
Singing	
Journal Insights	
Diagramming/ Analogy	
Personal Translation	

Appendix 3

Journal of Biblical Meditation

Scripture	
Slow Repetition	
Memorization	
Study	
Personalize	
Confessing	
Praying	
Envisioning	
Singing	
Journal Insights	
Diagramming/ Analogy	
Personal Translation	

Journal of Biblical Meditation

Scripture	
Slow Repetition	
Memorization	
Study	
Personalize	
Confessing	
Praying	
Envisioning	
Singing	
Journal Insights	
Diagramming/ Analogy	
Personal Translation	

Appendix 3

Journal of Biblical Meditation

Scripture	
Slow Repetition	
Memorization	
Study	
Personalize	
Confessing	
Praying	
Envisioning	
Singing	
Journal Insights	
Diagramming/ Analogy	
Personal Translation	

Journal of Biblical Meditation

Scripture	
Slow Repetition	
Memorization	
Study	
Personalize	
Confessing	
Praying	
Envisioning	
Singing	
Journal Insights	
Diagramming/ Analogy	
Personal Translation	

Appendix 4

Genesis 3:1-7 - *Now the serpent was more crafty than any beast of the field which the LORD God had made. And he said to the woman, "Indeed, has God said, 'You shall not eat from any tree of the garden'?" The woman said to the serpent, "From the fruit of the trees of the garden we may eat; but from the fruit of the tree which is in the middle of the garden, God has said, 'You shall not eat from it or touch it, or you will die.'" The serpent said to the woman, "You surely will not die! For God knows that in the day you eat from it your eyes will be opened, and you will be like God, knowing good and evil." When the woman saw that the tree was good for food, and that it was a delight to the eyes, and that the tree was desirable to make one wise, she took from its fruit and ate; and she gave also to her husband with her, and he ate. Then the eyes of both of them were opened, and they knew that they were naked; and they sewed fig leaves together and made themselves loin coverings.*

Journal of Biblical Meditation

Scripture	
Slow Repetition	
Memorization	
Study	
Personalize	
Confessing	
Praying	
Envisioning	
Singing	
Journal Insights	
Diagramming/ Analogy	
Personal Translation	

Appendix 4

Journal of Biblical Meditation

Scripture	
Slow Repetition	
Memorization	
Study	
Personalize	
Confessing	
Praying	
Envisioning	
Singing	
Journal Insights	
Diagramming/ Analogy	
Personal Translation	

Journal of Biblical Meditation

Scripture	
Slow Repetition	
Memorization	
Study	
Personalize	
Confessing	
Praying	
Envisioning	
Singing	
Journal Insights	
Diagramming/ Analogy	
Personal Translation	

Appendix 4

Journal of Biblical Meditation

Scripture	
Slow Repetition	
Memorization	
Study	
Personalize	
Confessing	
Praying	
Envisioning	
Singing	
Journal Insights	
Diagramming/ Analogy	
Personal Translation	

Journal of Biblical Meditation

Scripture	
Slow Repetition	
Memorization	
Study	
Personalize	
Confessing	
Praying	
Envisioning	
Singing	
Journal Insights	
Diagramming/ Analogy	
Personal Translation	

Appendix 4

Journal of Biblical Meditation

Scripture	
Slow Repetition	
Memorization	
Study	
Personalize	
Confessing	
Praying	
Envisioning	
Singing	
Journal Insights	
Diagramming/ Analogy	
Personal Translation	

Journal of Biblical Meditation

Scripture	
Slow Repetition	
Memorization	
Study	
Personalize	
Confessing	
Praying	
Envisioning	
Singing	
Journal Insights	
Diagramming/ Analogy	
Personal Translation	

How to Use This Book

There are five ways that this material was designed for use. Originally it was to be used as an Intensive Discipleship material for small groups of men or women to help them move significantly forward in their Christian lives. It can also be used for a personal devotion, mentor-directed study, a class format, or a sermon series with small groups. I have outlined how this could be conducted.

Small Group Study

1. Ask three to five people to join you in doing this study. Participate in a small-group program within your church in which people are assigned to your small group to cover this material or develop your own group.

2. Set aside an hour to an hour and a half each week (or each month) to do the three crucial things required for spiritual life-change. First, discuss what happened when you practiced the spiritual exercises in the previous lesson. Second, learn about the next set of exercises and information. Third, take personal prayer requests from each member. This can often be most effective if it is done at breakfast or lunch in a restaurant before or during the workday. It doesn't have to be at church. In fact, many times it is better if it is not.

3. The time should be divided into three sections.

   a. The first 20-30 minutes should be spent sharing what happened when each person practiced the spiritual exercises that were assigned. Everyone must share even if they do not think that they were successful.

   b. The second 10-30 minutes are spent in learning the next week or month's lessons and exercises.

   c. The final 10-30 minutes are spent taking prayer requests from everyone. The prayer requests must be about the person themselves. This is not the time to have the group pray for a family member.

4. Each member of the group can read the book for further understanding of the information and exercises. The time spent together is not primarily a presentation time.

5. If one or more of the people have not tried or mastered the exercises, then the leader should feel free to repeat the same lesson again and again until this spiritual exercise is mastered.

6. If the group is meeting monthly rather than weekly, then more exercises are assigned. It can be helpful to have some form of accountability set up to make sure people are working on the exercises. This may be a daily or weekly e-mail stating what exercise they tried. The full explanation will come in the group time; but if everybody e-mails or texts what they are doing, then everybody stays on track.

How To Use This Book

Let's take a look at the first small group meeting:

1. Let everyone introduce themselves. A 60-second bio is usually helpful and lets everyone get to know everyone else.

2. Open in prayer.

3. Introduce the topic you will be exploring and pass out the books. Give an overview of the whole series.

4. Explain the first week or month's exercises.

5. Save 10-20 minutes for personal prayer requests.

The key to an effective discipleship group is not what the teacher says; it is what the disciple does. So give each person lots of time to tell about what happened when he or she started to practice the discipline. If the people in the group did not adequately try the discipline or did not see results from trying the discipline, then spend another week on that discipline. The goal of the group is not to get through the material within a specific amount of time but to develop new spiritual habits that will change their lives.

Personal Devotional Study

A second way to use this material is as a personal devotional study. In this format you can work through the material and look up the verses on your own, taking notes, practicing the exercises, and writing down your experiences for personal review. In this type of study proceed at your own pace. It may be one chapter a week, or it may be one chapter a day. The key is that the information is digested and the exercises are tried until some level of mastery is accomplished. It can be helpful to share your progress in this material with a mentor or spiritual accountability partner.

Let's take a look at what a personal devotional study would look like:

1. Open in prayer.
2. Read the material in the chapter.
3. Practice the exercise(s) suggested.
4. Record what you did, what happened when you did it, and what you continue to do because of using this exercise.
5. Practice the exercise again or in a different way until mastered.

How To Use This Book

Mentor-Directed Study

One of the most powerful ways of using this material is to ask a respected Christian you know to mentor you through this material. They do not need to do the study with you, but they do need to monitor and encourage you in the process of this study.

1. Ask a mentor to listen to your progress through this material once a month and pray for you as you explore these issues and exercises.

2. Meet the first time with your mentor and purchase a book for them so they can be tracking your progress. This meeting could be at a restaurant or a coffee house so that the meeting is more informal.

   a. Let them know what you are hoping to accomplish with this study and at what speed you would like to move through the material.

   b. Give them the freedom to teach, correct, rebuke, and train you as you move through the material (2 Timothy 3:16).

   c. Agree to meet monthly or weekly to hear updates on how you are doing. Remember, this is about you and not about them. They are mentoring you through this material and may not be going through it themselves. They are your spiritual guide, not a co-laborer.

   d. Have your mentor watch you pray or practice the exercise as they watch. They may be able to suggest ways to more effectively practice the spiritual exercise.

3. Ask your mentor to follow the following format for your monthly or weekly sessions:

   a. Spend 20-30 minutes listening to what you have done and experienced as you have worked through the exercises.

   b. Listen to their insights and additions.

   c. Spend 10-20 minutes as they assign and explore the next chapter or re-assign the current material because they think there is a need to dwell on these ideas or habits more thoroughly.

   d. Spend 10-20 minutes giving the mentor three specific personal prayer requests you would like them to pray for until the next meeting.

4. Realize that your mentor may want to move off in tangents that are not directly tied to the material in this study guide, but that is what you want. They have life experience and spiritual wisdom that you want to be poured into your life. A mentor can often see mistakes or missteps that are about to take place when we cannot see them. Also, mentors can listen for the emotional, psychological, or spiritual pain that we have not been able to talk about before.

How To Use This Book

Class Format

A fourth way to use this material is in a class or mid-week teaching time at the church. The material that is contained in the book can be presented to a class, but it should take only about half the time allowed for the class. The other half of the time should be used for small groups to discuss what happened the week before when the discipline was tried. Also, allow for questions and prayer requests in regard to a growing spiritual life. This material should be repeated regularly as a part of a church's ongoing discipleship strategy. Every year or every other year a church can run one of these classes so that people are moving forward.

The greatest danger to using this material in a class setting is that the teacher will use the whole time to present the material, not allowing adequate discussion of what happened when it was tried.

Second, there is the danger that it will be offered as new information only rather than as new practices or habits to incorporate into their life. The value of this material is in the exercises, not in the information. It is not possible to have a consistently deep walk with God without some of these disciplines being a part of their life. These materials are not just for delivering new information; they are to be practiced.

A third danger in using this material in a classroom setting is that the teacher or facilitator may not feel the freedom to repeat a discipline until all in the class have adequately tried it. There needs to be the freedom to go back over material that is not fully embraced until it has been adequately explored.

Let's take a look at what using this material in a classroom setting would look like:

Advertise the class in various places at church, work, or community. For the first classroom period let's take a look at what the first meeting of the classroom setting would look like:

1. Open in prayer.

2. Introduce an overview of the topic and pass out the books.

3. Let people know that this is an exercise/application-focused group, not a new information-focused group. They will learn new information but only so that they can then apply it to their life.

4. Introduce the first few exercises that will be tried in the first week or month.

5. Break the group into small groups for personal prayer requests.

How To Use This Book

For the remaining class periods, the following is the format for the standard meeting:

1. Open in prayer.

2. Give people 10-30 minutes to break into small groups of three or four and tell each other how the exercises from the last meeting went.

3. Spend 10-30 minutes explaining the new concepts and exercises to the group.

4. Put the group back into their small groups for personal prayer requests. Everybody has to share something that they want everyone to pray about.

Sermon Series and Small Groups

A fifth way to use this material is as a sermon series with accompanying small groups. This is where the whole church listens to the sermon series that the pastor is preaching, and then all small groups practice the material by doing the spiritual workouts at the end of each chapter. This is really a lab-lecture model of discipleship. It can be quite effective if the small group allows people to talk about trying the various disciplines. This is a way to jump-start Sunday morning attenders into people who are serious about developing spiritual habits. This multi-pronged approach can be very effective if there is adequate planning and opportunity for new groups to form even after the sermon series has started.

The goal of this book is that many Christians will begin practicing their Christianity and experiencing new levels of closeness with God. The process of walking with Christ takes time. The addition of new habits of life is essential. Expect that some will try these disciplines and then stop. Expect that others will have been waiting for this material for a long time and can quickly push to new depths with God. Patiently persevere. You and others will reap great joy in the presence of God.

About the Author

Gil Stieglitz is a catalyst for positive change both personally and organizationally. He excites, educates, and motivates audiences all over the world through passion, humor, leadership, and wisdom. He has led seminars in China, Europe, Canada, Mexico, and all over the United States.

Since founding the nonprofit ministry Principles to Live By in 1992 to help people and organizations win at life through Biblical Wisdom, Dr. Gil has been asked to repair, lead, and reinvigorate numerous organizations and individuals. He successfully led a church to 1400% growth in a disadvantaged area. As a Denominational Superintendent in the Western United States he led 50 churches and 250 pastors to over 300% growth. As a Superintendent of Schools he oversaw a school system as it doubled in 4 years. As an executive pastor at a mega-church he rebuilt a staff and added over a 1,000 people. He injects dynamic life-change as a professor at universities and graduate schools on the West Coast and through seminars, sermons, and lecture series. He also partners with Courage Worldwide which rescues young girls who have been forced into sexual slavery in America.

He has a B.A. from Biola University, a Master's Degree and a Doctorate in Christian Leadership from Talbot School of Theology. He has authored over two dozen books, manuals, and development courses including three best sellers. Dr. Gil's resources are available at Amazon.com as well as at www.PrinciplesToLiveBy.com.

Gil and his wife, Dana, have enjoyed over twenty-five years of marriage and reside in Roseville, California, where they raised their three precious girls.

Other Resources by Gil Stieglitz

Becoming Courageous

Breakfast with Solomon Volume 1

Breakfast with Solomon Volume 2

Breakfast with Solomon Volume 3

Breaking Satanic Bondage

Deep Happiness: The Eight Secrets

Delighting in God

Delighting in Jesus

Developing a Christian Worldview

God's Radical Plan for Husbands

God's Radical Plan for Wives

Going Deep In Prayer: 40 Days of In-Depth Prayer

Leading a Thriving Ministry

Marital Intelligence

Mission Possible: Winning the Battle Over Temptation

Proverbs: A Devotional Commentary Volume 1

Secrets of God's Armor

Spiritual Disciplines of a C.H.R.I.S.T.I.A.N

They Laughed When I Wrote Another Book About Prayer, Then They Read It

Touching the Face of God: 40 Days of Adoring God

Why There Has to Be a Hell

Podcasts

Becoming a Godly Parent

Biblical Meditation: The Keys of Transformation

Everyday Spiritual Warfare Series

God's Guide to Handling Money

Spiritual War Surrounding Money

The Four Keys to a Great Family

The Ten Commandments

If you would be interested in having Gil Stieglitz speak to your group, you can contact Him through the website

www.ptlb.com

www.ingramcontent.com/pod-product-compliance
Lightning Source LLC
Chambersburg PA
CBHW032120090426
42743CB00007B/408